1985

Malpractice

Malpractice

A Guide to the Legal Rights of Patients and Doctors

DONALD J. FLASTER, M.D., LL. B.

Charles Scribner's Sons • New York

Copyright © 1983 Donald J. Flaster

Library of Congress Cataloging in Publication Data

Flaster, Donald J.
    Malpractice: a guide to the legal rights of patients
and doctors.

    Includes index.
    1. Physicians—Malpractice—United States.
I. Title.
KF2905.3.F58   1983   346.7303'32   83-3426
ISBN 0-684-17903-2   347.306332

1 3 5 7 9 11 13 15 17 19   F/C   20 18 16 14 12 10 8 6 4 2

Printed in the United States of America.

To all those patients who have been wronged by
slipshod, incompetent, or uncaring doctors . . .
And to all those doctors who have been victimized
by unfeeling and greedy patients
This book is dedicated in the hope that it may
bring about better mutual understanding
and benefit both parties.

CONTENTS

PREFACE

It can be argued that we are in the midst of a malpractice crisis. Crisis or no, the number of lawsuits filed against medical doctors continues to increase, with a few juries awarding sums that begin to sound like the national debt.

A generation ago, the relationship between doctor and patient was routinely regarded as intimate and precious. What happened to make them adversaries, to make antagonism more common than empathy and understanding? Who is at fault—the legal profession, patients, or doctors?

This book analyzes the situation from all sides. If you have considered suing your doctor, the book will help you to examine your reasons, determine whether you have a valid case, and proceed in the most efficient manner. You will learn why certain doctors are especially prone to suits while others in the same specialty go through their careers with hardly a threat of legal action against them.

As a physician and attorney, and now a consultant using both disciplines, I have had many opportunities to observe the crisis from both sides, to see with the clarity of the disinterested third person why patients sue and why some doctors are sued. In some instances, both patient and doctor appear justified in their actions; in others, neither is justified. And some cases are promoted by attorneys who thrive on frequent litigation, retaining as much as 50 percent of anything recovered for the client.

Besides the unpleasant subject of malpractice litigation, I discuss the changing relationship between doctors and their patients and focus on the rights of patients as contrasted with the mere courtesies extended by the nicer doctors. My hope is to give you a better understanding of your doctor, a better relationship with him or her if possible, and a clearer knowledge of how you might go about being compensated if your doctor fails to meet acceptable standards.

CHAPTER 1

WHAT IS MALPRACTICE?

JUST WHAT IS IT?

The word *malpractice* has no specific legal meaning. It is, rather, a term of common usage that refers to certain types of misconduct or improper performance of professional duties by the physician (or other professional), for which he or she becomes legally liable to compensate a patient who is the victim of this wrongful act.

But what is a wrongful act? If you contract for a new roof on your house and it leaks after being installed, you have suffered a wrongful act and a failure to fulfill your rightful expectations from the roofing contractor. We expect, and have every right to expect, that the purpose of a roof is to keep the elements from entering a building from above. If the roof leaks, the person who installed it has performed incompetently. If you purchase a vacuum cleaner that fails to pick up even simple dust from your floor or carpet, the manufacturer or salesperson has com-

1

mitted a wrongful act in representing that the cleaner will, in fact, clean.

But if you visit a physician seeking a cure for an illness, and despite the physician's efforts your symptoms persist, is the physician guilty of negligence or malpractice? Has the doctor committed a wrongful act? That may be the case, but it is not necessarily so. More facts are needed to form an opinion in such matters.

A physician is held to a standard of performance representative of accepted professional skills, but not all physicians are held to the same level of performance. A general practitioner is not expected to be as knowledgeable about the fine points of cardiac diagnosis or treatment as the cardiologist who has trained for as many as six additional years in this special field.

Do we expect the family doctor in a rural farm area or a wilderness area to be as knowledgeable about the latest developments in medical care as the specialist in internal medicine, or even the general practitioner, who practices in New York City or Los Angeles with daily access to the world's leading experts and a never-ending succession of postgraduate educational programs? The answer is usually, but not always. If the diagnosis is acute appendicitis, whose symptoms are taught to Boy Scouts and Girl Scouts, the answer is yes. If, on the other hand, the problem turns out to be an obscure disease about which little is known, and only a few isolated cases of which are seen in the course of a year, the answer is certainly not. Even the suspicion of such a disease would be a remarkable accomplishment on the part of the general practitioner, rural or urban. It is not the "standard of care" to which such a doctor can be held reasonably, considering the level of training and experience required to perform as a general practitioner. The doctor who does, finally, suspect the obscure disease should probably be rewarded for unexpected diligence, not sued for not having thought of it sooner.

Though few people any longer receive *free* medical care as "charity cases"—various federal and state government medical care programs usually compensate the physician— the fact that a patient is a charity case does not in any way alter the doctor's duty to practice the profession at acceptable standards. The fact that he or she received no compensation for services is no defense or excuse for inferior care.

The general rule the courts apply to determine if malpractice has been committed is to ask: Has this doctor performed in a manner consistent with his educational level and training, and in a manner consistent with the work of doctors of similar education and training in the community? In recent years, with the great advances in communications and travel, there has been a tendency by the courts to disregard the "community" clause or "locality rule." Some courts have declared that even the rural doctor has ready access to medical publications and educational meetings, and though it might be more inconvenient for a rural doctor than for his big-city cousin, nonetheless the obligation to keep abreast of new developments in medicine is the same.

MALPRACTICE, OR TREATMENT FAILURE?

As noted above, a doctor's failure to relieve your symptoms or cure your disease *may* be malpractice, but is not necessarily so. What, then, are the criteria for malpractice? And are there exceptions to these criteria?

Despite giant leaps forward in medical treatment in the past thirty years or so, medicine remains a most complex and baffling science. Every part and system of the human body interacts constantly with every other part and system, and no two individuals are exactly alike at any given moment. Doctors must also consider their patients' vast differences in behavior, personality, diet, heredity, and activity while trying to reach a diagnosis. Add finally a list of medications, prescribed or purchased at the supermarket or pharmacy, different for every individual, and we have still greater disparity.

Into this hodgepodge of factors a doctor pours a medication with which he or she is intimately familiar, one that will, under normal circumstances and in the proper dose, relieve your symptoms or cure your illness. Surprise, it doesn't work! Is the doctor negligent? Has *malpractice* been committed?

More answers are needed. Did the doctor question you about any and all other medications you might have been taking at the time, or which you are in the habit of taking occasionally, including things you might consider unimportant or irrelevant, such as aspirin, cold preparations, cough medicines, nonprescription sleeping pills, diet pills, water pills, oral contraceptives, or fertility pills? Did you remember to tell the doctor about every single one of them? Or did you perhaps forget to mention the water pills you take every month for your premenstrual bloating, and which, unbeknownst to you, might cause a bad reaction when administered together with certain prescription drugs?

Did the doctor give you specific instructions, beyond just the dosage, for taking the medicine? Taking some antibiotics just before or too close to a meal, for example, may cause the antibiotic to bind to certain minerals in the food and become totally unavailable to fight your infection. Medications interact in strange ways, sometimes antagonizing each other's actions, sometimes *enhancing* them. In the latter case, a normal dose could become an overdose when taken with another medication that increases its potency. Your doctor, not you, must know when such interactions are possible, and should question you about the use of other medications, especially those that might interact with the one he intends to prescribe for you. If your doctor did not ask, he may have committed malpractice. If your doctor asked and can prove it, but you neglected to answer, malpractice has not been committed.

Your seeking medical assistance, and your physician's agreement to examine and prescribe for you, does not constitute a contract in which the doctor promises to cure you. Your doctor does agree to try his best, and represents that this effort is consistent with that expected of other physicians with the same level of training and education. Your part of this "contract" is to give complete and truthful information, and to permit the doctor to examine your body and to conduct certain tests upon it that appear necessary, not only in order to make the correct diagnosis but also to rule out other ailments that have similar symptoms and might confuse the diagnosis.

If you call a doctor to report that your thirteen-year-old daughter has severe abdominal pain with nausea and vomiting, and the doctor suggests that it is probably a virus and offers to phone in a prescription to your pharmacist, but the illness turns out to be acute appendicitis, your doctor has been negligent in not insisting on examining the child. It is no secret that these are the symptoms of appendicitis, and that the disease is most common in this age group. It is also well known that acute appendicitis requires immediate emergency surgery, and that delay can result in serious consequences.

But suppose your doctor *had* asked to examine the child but *you* insisted on the telephone prescription, perhaps to save the visit fee. A truly concerned physician should have *refused to comply* with your request. If your doctor did comply, the blame still lies with him. The physician, not you, is the one expected to "know better." If you flatly refused to bring the child in for a proper examination, you have taken the blame upon yourself, and a later suit for malpractice is not justified. If the doctor has a written record of the conversation, or a witness who has heard the attempts to convince you of the need for the examination, you could not win your suit.

There are some *exceptions,* and one deserves particular attention. One type of medical care *is* considered to be a legal contract; one type of doctor is viewed under the law as having *guaranteed* results—the plastic surgeon who performs cosmetic surgery. If you tell a plastic surgeon "I want a nose like *that,*" presenting a clear photograph of your dream nose, and the surgeon agrees to reshape your own proboscis into the desired shape, the surgeon has contracted with you for a specific job. If the nose turns out other than what you wanted, you have a case, but not a case of negligence. This is simple breach of contract—as with the roofer. Such suits may be one reason for plastic surgeons' high fees.

MALPRACTICE, OR ABANDONMENT?

Your husband takes ill suddenly, and you call a nearby physician you have never visited before, who refuses to see your husband. Is the doctor negligent?

Professional ethics suggest that the physician should be available to the sick upon request, but no law *compels* a doctor to take on any patient, at any time, for any reason. The doctor *is* obliged, however, to continue treatment once he begins the relationship either by discussing the symptoms or examining the patient. But the physician need not take on a new patient, or even accept a former patient whom the doctor has not seen recently and has never treated for the present illness. The law recognizes the establishment of a doctor–patient relationship even when the relationship is based only on a telephone conversation in which the doctor has discussed the symptoms with the patient or another person speaking for any patient too sick or too young or whatever to talk for himself. Even though no direct physical contact has taken place, even though the doctor has not *seen* or examined the patient, the doctor is considered to have entered the case and to have established a doctor–patient relationship on the basis of a detailed discussion of the symptoms. The doctor may not now brush the patient off. If he does, and some serious complication or death occurs, and is judged to be due at least in part to the fact that the doctor did not follow through on the earlier conversation, the doctor is liable. Simple conversations, however, in which only a very superficial mention of the problem is followed by a refusal by the doctor to see the patient, usually do not signify that a relationship has been established. The doctor is not then deemed to have abandoned the sick person.

A doctor might refuse to see your husband for a *new* illness because you haven't paid your bills in the past. The doctor is within his rights so long as there is no detailed discussion of the symptoms. If the matter ever comes into court, however, the physician would have to show that he did not have your husband under continuing treatment for this illness, that the last visit was a long time ago, and that he had never discussed with your husband any symptoms that might have suggested that such an illness was imminent or developing.

But what if your doctor is really fed up with you and your continual refusal to follow instructions and to return for follow-up visits? Your doctor wants to be rid of you as a patient; you have become a frustration, and are casting aspersions on his professional reputation. Does your doctor have recourse? Yes, indeed. Your doctor can simply inform you (preferably by certified mail) that he no longer desires to be responsible for your medical care and suggests that you place yourself under the care of another physician, because in the doctor's opinion you *do* need further care, and that he will remain available to you for a reasonable and specified period of time before you find another doctor. Though the "reasonable" length of time varies with the nature of the illness, a week or two is usually considered sufficient. When the specified time runs out, your doctor is free of you and bears no further responsibility for your care. If an acute emergency occurs and you are without care because you neglected to find another doctor, your former doctor cannot be held legally responsible.

If you are under a doctor's care, even if you are in a hospital, and he goes off for a day, a weekend, or even a two-week vacation, your doctor has *not* abandoned you if he has provided a licensed and qualified physician of similar training and education as a substitute. Your doctor need not inform you of the substitution in advance, and it doesn't matter if you don't like the substitute doctor as much as your own. No abandonment has been committed. Furthermore, if your doctor feels that your condition requires the care of a specialist or an expert in another field, and you have no other condition that requires treatment, your own doctor need not continue to care for you once the other doctor has, with your agreement, taken charge of the case.

Patients frequently complain that their own family doctor did not visit them daily when they were hospitalized, under the care of a surgeon, for an operation. Yet these same patients are often the first to howl bitterly if the family doctor *does* make daily visits just to say hello and then submits a bill, to the patient or the insurance carrier, for "daily hospital visits." Look into your heart most carefully: which way would you prefer? Tell your family doctor your decision at the outset, and both of you will be happier. If you say nothing, the doctor must make the choice, and from where he stands, trying it first one way with one patient, then the other way with the next, he feels that he is "wrong" however he handles the situation.

Strictly speaking, a doctor who stops at the scene of an accident to render assistance to the injured is required to maintain supervision of the patient *until another physician takes over*. If the doctor looks after you only until you are safely placed into the ambulance by the local volunteer first-aid squad, technically *the doctor has abandoned you.* The training or competence (or lack of same) of the first-aid squad or ambulance attendants is immaterial, unless they continue the care of the injured or ill person under direct orders of a physician with whom they are in contact via two-way radio. Most people are familiar with such situations from the popular television show "Emergency."

What do you think of when you hear the words "assault and battery"? Like most people, you probably think of mugging or some other form of physical attack. But did you know that the doctor who stopped to assist you by the roadside, without first identifying himself and getting your *permission* to examine you and render assistance, has, under the old law, committed assault and battery? So many accident victims have later sued the passing doctor who stopped at the scene to render first aid that all states have now passed good samaritan laws. These laws provide that a physician (the good samaritan) who stops at the scene of an accident to give assistance to the injured may no longer be sued for either abandonment or assault. In some states these laws cover only a doctor who stops at the scene of an accident to render aid. In others, the law extends to any passerby who helps. But all of the laws cover only charges of aassault and abandonment. What about malpractice?

Regardless of the circumstances, the physician is still expected to render quality care, and to exhibit the standard of competence expected in the performance of professional duties. An improperly placed tourniquet or splint may be only an unfortunate mistake if applied by a first-aid squad member or passerby, but it is professional negligence when applied by a physician. Naturally, a doctor cannot do as fine a job by the side of a highway with the aid of a flashlight as is possible in a fully equipped emergency room. Nevertheless, if incompetent care is rendered and results in permanent injury to you, you cannot sue the first-aid squad for malpractice. You can sue the doctor.

In situations where the doctor, or substitute doctor, who admits you to a hospital fails to visit you for an unreasonable period of time, or fails to visit you at reasonable intervals consistent with proper care of your illness, you may have the basis for a lawsuit. For example, if your doctor orders you into the hospital, then fails to come in to see you for three or four days, this may be considered abandonment. If you are suffering from an acute (rapidly changing) illness (a coronary or diabetic coma, to name two common examples) and your doctor only visits once or twice a week, this is not consistent with the expected standards of care. If visits are made by a substitute physician of equivalent training (another cardiologist or diabetologist, for instance), the requirements for proper care have been met. If your physician leaves you in the hands of a resident (the hospital-employed doctor in training), the requirements for proper care have not been met unless you were admitted to a public or teaching hospital as a "service" case (you didn't specify your own physician or surgeon), and it was made clear to you that the in-hospital staff, and not your private physician, would take care of and assume responsibility for you. Of course, the resident physicians are under the supervision of fully qualified full-time hospital staff members who may also be the professors of medicine at the affiliated medical school.

The resident staff may provide you with interim care *between* visits of your own doctor, but your doctor is obliged to visit at reasonable intervals. The determination of "reasonable" depends on the nature of your illness.

MALPRACTICE, OR HUMAN ERROR?

There exists a very fine line between that which constitutes a wrongful professional act, an inadequate or incompetent treatment or diagnosis, and what is simply a human error or unanticipated result that occurs despite the best efforts of the doctor acting in a most professional manner. Generally, malpractice can be properly evaluated only by other physicians, and most commonly the evaluation requires a courtroom trial in which doctors appear as expert witnesses to testify for both sides, leaving the judge or jury to determine whose arguments are more convincing.

My teenage offspring like to remind me that "nobody's perfect." There exists a wide margin between those oversights in medical management that occur in the course of the most diligent treatment, and those glaring errors that simply would not have occurred had competent attention been paid by the doctor. It is these errors that we call negligence or malpractice, and that may form the basis of future lawsuits. Human error is just that: *human* error. A forgotten bit of significant medical history or a mixing of incompatible medications that is promptly stopped before any harm has been done when the physician realizes the mistake are elements of human error, not malpractice. Some injury must result from the error or oversight before malpractice becomes compensable. If the error caused you no injury or extra expense, and was quickly reversed as soon as it was identified, the courts are highly unlikely to grant you a monetary award.

In the courtroom everything is either black or white. A defendant is innocent or guilty, liable or not liable. But in the world of medicine, many shades of gray are evident, and uncertainty is more common than absolute fact or resolution. The accuracy of a diagnosis is often confounded by other medical or physical conditions that exist concurrently, or by symptoms that are unclear as they are described by you to the doctor. Even so relatively simple a matter as acute appendicitis rarely presents itself with the classic textbook picture, which is really nothing more than an average composite clinical picture painted from the many variations. During my years in practice, I only saw one case of "textbook" appendicitis that required no thought or weighing of various factors before I decided to recommend emergency surgery rather than diligent observation. The case was that of my own daughter.

MALPRACTICE, OR MISINFORMATION?

If a failure of communication, which is to say that the physician's explanation of your illness or the proposed treatment was incomplete, or was only partially or inaccurately understood by you, leaves you unprepared for a poor treatment result or an unexpected side effect, malpractice *may* have been committed. Here, once again, the decision is not clear-cut, but must be rendered by a court. The patient's consent for treatment is absolutely essential, and failure to obtain it may lead to serious consequences for the physician. The consent must be based on the patient's understanding of valid and complete information, not just a cursory expression of faith in the doctor's judgment. Lack of "informed consent" is the basis of many malpractice suits. This subject will be addressed in greater detail in the next chapter, when the whole subject of informed consent is taken up, and again in Chapter 4.

MALPRACTICE, OR DID YOU JUST EXPECT TOO MUCH?

Suppose you bring a serious problem to your family doctor and insist that you want only him to handle it. Not being a specialist in the field, he is not quite up to the task, though he tries his best to accommodate you. Before concluding that his failure to achieve satisfactory results is malpractice, you must honestly ask yourself: "Did I expect too much of him?". As discussed earlier in this chapter, every doctor is expected to measure up to a certain minimum level of competence. After all, he did go through four years of medical school, probably at least one additional year of hospital training, and pass a difficult licensing examination. But not every physician is expected to know the fine points of diagnosis and treatment in every area of medicine. Certain specialists have been through as many as six or more years of additional training and have passed another very difficult examination (specialty "Boards"). Those without this additional education, training, and experience may not be as adept as a specialist at the intricacies of distinguishing between two similar illnesses or the delicate balancing of treatment of two coexistent illnesses for which the indicated medications conflict. Still, the generalist has a *broadness* of training and experience that cannot be matched by any specialist. His continuing care of you and your family over a prolonged period of years ("from womb to tomb" is the private term among doctors) builds up a level of understanding that cannot be found in the specialist to whom you go perhaps once in a lifetime with a special problem, or who only addresses himself to one of your problems. Both the generalist and the specialist have a most distinct role, and neither should be viewed as a second-class member of the profession or inferior to the other.

MALPRACTICE, OR DID YOU HAVE SOMETHING ELSE IN MIND?

Statistics show that more than 80 percent of all malpractice suits that are filed never come to trial, and lawyers experienced in malpractice cases refuse to take on many patients' complaints because the cases clearly have no merit. Some suits are settled out of court, but the majority are simply dropped somewhere along the way. This suggests that these cases had no initial basis in fact and were filed during a period of frustration and anger directed toward the doctor for a variety of reasons that will be examined more closely in the next chapter.

Some patients want, quite simply, to avoid paying the doctor's bill. It is well known that to avoid further inflaming the patient and the situation, insurance companies and their lawyers tell doctors that they should not pursue a heavy-handed collection effort against a patient who has filed suit. By the time the case is dropped, the patient hopes that the doctor will forget or write off the bill. But financial obligations are not always avoided quite that easily. We will see in a later chapter how best to handle the matter of outstanding bills when contemplating a malpractice suit.

Of course, a single lawsuit could have multiple allegations. A doctor could, for example, be accused simultaneously of negligence, of having performed medical procedures without getting the proper informed consent of the patient, and of abandonment, and could be found guilty of one, several, or all of the charges when the final verdict is rendered. But these are legal details, and the choice of specific charges to be listed in the suit is best made by your attorney, based on the information you have supplied or which emerges during preparation of the suit.

Now that you have a clearer picture of what malpractice is and what it probably is not, in Chapter 2 we will examine the motivations and reasons that lead a patient to sue a doctor. Only you can look into your mind and thoughts and decide what has made you consider filing a lawsuit against a doctor. Only you know if the suit appears justified or not. If it is justified, you are entitled to redress for the wrong done to you. If not, you would do well to read carefully the information in Chapter 7 in order to better understand the effects your lawsuit may have on the doctor, and on his or her relations with other patients.

CHAPTER 2

WHO SUES, AND WHY?

YOUR AVERAGE PLAINTIFF

He or she may or may not be rich, but is not likely to be poor, for the lower socioeconomic classes traditionally do not bring suit for any reason. Most likely of all, your average plaintiff belongs to the somewhat sophisticated, educated, socially aware middle class.

Mr. or Ms. Average Plaintiff is up-to-date on the material in the press, the news media, and the book lists that now offer self-help instruction on medical diagnosis and treatment as easily as they produce how-to books, articles, and TV special reports on fixing cars, remodeling homes, or equaling the culinary skills of the finest chefs. I recently saw an advertisement for a self-help book that claimed that it "helps the layperson diagnose an illness as the professionals do: by looking up the symptoms."

They listen avidly to the advice of medical experts seen

often on TV, assuming the very general advice given by these knowledgeable persons can be applied specifically to the individual viewer's problem when, in fact, if the advice is applicable, it is only by chance. They read the medical columns in *Good Housekeeping, McCalls, Reader's Digest,* and *Time* magazine. Their home library is as likely to contain how-to books on medicine as it is to have a copy of the writings of Socrates, Hemingway, or even Shakespeare.

But *knowledge* alone does not create malpractice suits. Some other factor or factors must come into play before Mr. or Ms. A.P. gets litigious, before he or she consults an attorney for the purpose of suing a doctor.

Can the patient evaluate the competence of the doctor? When members of my own family diagnosed or medicated themselves, I would remind them that the fifteen years I spent studying medicine must have resulted in my acquiring *some* more knowledge than they had about these matters. I would chide my father for believing that he had acquired *two* medical degrees (one for me, one for himself) for the price of only one tuition fee. I cautioned my wife that close association with me did not impart my medical judgment to her through some mysterious intercorporeal process of absorption. The only truly valid evaluation of a physician's competence and performance is made by other physicians, who can best appreciate the fine points and the extenuating circumstances of a specific medical situation. And at times they can't even agree among themselves!

The physician understands that total objectivity is necessary for the proper care of a patient. It is for this very reason that doctors rarely take care of their own spouses or children. They know only too well, and fear, that emotional involvement will cloud their judgment, and that subjective judgments have a subconscious tendency to ignore ominous signs and symptoms that might be suggestive of serious diseases. We don't want to see them, so we don't see them. We ask a colleague to take over. Now, if the doctor cannot objectively evaluate an illness in his own immediate family, how can the nonphysician *patient* do so? The patient not only lacks the objectivity, but all but the most superficial veneer of medical knowledge and information. And regardless of how much "medical" reading you do, or how "complete and unabridged" your home medical care book is supposed to be, you have not acquired any depth of medical knowledge, and none of the visual, auditory, and tactile skills that are so essential to physical examination. In medicine, for every "fact," there are fifty "buts," "maybes," and extenuating circumstances that may send the thinking process off in a totally new direction. Such judgments do not come from self-help books or TV specials.

Confronted with a medical case for the first time, a physician takes a medical "history" (questions the patient about present and past signs and symptoms), formulates additional specific questions based in part on the answers to the previous ones, and finally selects a most likely diagnosis, followed by a list (which may be lengthy indeed) of other possible illnesses that might have a similar clinical picture and must therefore be ruled out. These are known as the "differential diagnoses." Examination of the patient will usually result in a final diagnosis. On occasion, the doctor will require the help of X rays, blood tests, cardiograms, and other such laboratory evaluations to find the true diagnosis. Diagnoses, however, are rarely made on the basis of laboratory tests alone. These tests are intended to confirm the doctor's judgment, not replace it. One joke that circulates among doctors goes: "I have the results of the forty-three blood tests I ordered, Mrs. Smith. They seem to indicate that your main problem is a severe loss of blood . . ." Sometimes the doctor uses such tests to prove the absence of other, more serious diseases for his or her own legal protection (against *you*).

Who is your average plaintiff? It can be you, your neighbor, or your friends. The only common denominator is that all of you may no longer be content with the services rendered by your doctor.

YOUR RELATIONSHIP WITH YOUR DOCTOR

Despite the very real loss of the close relationship between many doctors and patients, most patients would subconsciously still like to view doctors as a father image (Mother image? We do have an ever-increasing number of highly competent female physicians), and doctors would dearly love to continue to play the role. In the past, this relationship helped patients to *feel* better even before they began to *get* better, and was variously known as the bedside manner, tending loving care (TLC), or the art of medicine (as distinguished from the *science* of medicine). The special relationship certainly made doctors feel good, and was the primary compensation for getting up at three in the morning, or spending an anniversary or a child's birthday at a patient's bedside during a critical illness. This, not money, was the real reason he (and I!) did it—in the old days, and even today, more often than most patients realize, or most doctors would ever admit. True, he earned a good living from it, but he also had gone without any significant earnings at all until the age of thirty or thirty-two and had a lot of catching up to do.

The word used to describe that special doctor–patient relationship, that feeling, is "empathy." The dictionary* defines empathy as "the capacity for participating in another's feelings." The doctor felt your pain, your discomfort, your suffering and that of your family. You felt the doctor's sympathy, the desire to help you, the frustration when the treatments known to science were inadequate. Physicians are often accused of "turning their backs" on

* *Webster's Third New International*, G. & C. Merriam, 1971.

the dying. It's a proper accusation, but few people understand that it results from the anger and frustration of having been defeated in the battle against death. The imminent demise of a patient is the ultimate failure for the doctor. The physician may "turn his back," may appear cold and uninterested, but he doesn't sleep too well that night, or the next.

Did you know that physicians make up the social group with the highest rate of depression and suicide? Did you know that the highest rate of marital difficulties and/or breakdowns occurs in doctors' families? It takes a very special woman to deal with him, and to accept the knowledge that she can only ever attain the number-two position in a physician's life, always behind some patient, some emergency. Doctors' children are notorious for their emotional disturbances, alcoholism, trouble with the law; their conclusion is that Daddy loves his patients more than he does them. But we have not yet answered the question "What happened to that relationship, that 'empathy'?"

The last time you called your doctor on a Wednesday, reached the answering service instead, and were referred to another doctor or the nearest emergency room, did you picture someone trying to revive a psyche worn down from the pressures and responsibilities of the past few days, or did you envision someone on a golf course, caring little if you were sick? When you saw your doctor drive by in a new car, did you think he or she was just showing off a status symbol, or did you consider the possibility that your doctor absolutely requires a 100 percent reliable, sturdy car that will never fail when needed most. ("I'm sorry your husband is having a heart attack, Mrs. Smith, but my jalopy is on the fritz again and won't be ready until Tuesday!") When my car began to show signs of frequent breakdown or "planned obsolescence" and I purchased a new one, my father used to say, "Now you look like a *real* doctor again!" (Was I a *fake* doctor while still driving the three-year-old car?)

There are those who claim that the single most important cause of the malpractice crisis is not the breakdown of the doctor–patient relationship or even the litigation-minded society in which we live, but the very widespread and generally *impersonal*, businesslike contacts the patient now has with those in the health professions that serve him or her. This is particularly notable in the hospital environment.

The anesthesiologist, a highly skilled professional who bears the responsibility for watching over the patient's life functions during surgery, is to you some vague person with whom you have only two recollectable contacts: a brief visit the night before surgery when anxiety and sedatives dim your appreciation, and the arrival of the bill in the mail. Most patients do not even recall their anesthesiologist's name. Florence Nightingales are hard to find among today's efficient but impersonal nursing staffs, and much of your visible contact is with nurses' aides for whom nursing is a job, not a professional service. Much of your in-hospital doctor contact, especially in teaching hospitals, is with a constantly rotating staff of doctors in training, and neither they nor you have the opportunity to form any sort of close relationship with the other.

The breakdown of the close emotional ties between patient and doctor is by no means one-sided. Your doctor now rarely looks after you for a lifetime, and your children from conception to marriage and beyond. Your doctor sees you now and again, often turns you over to a specialist in another field (if you haven't already gone there on your own), and may share your care with many specialists. You engage an obstetrician for your pregnancy (depriving your family doctor of what was my most enjoyable act: presenting you with your newborn child); a pediatrician for routine examinations of the child; an allergist for your hay fever; an orthopedic surgeon for the sprained ankle your son suffered falling off his skateboard; a gastroenterologist for your husband's ulcer; and a psychiatrist or a psychologist to discuss the marital problems, or guilt feelings you experienced when you had to put a senile parent into a nursing home. You self-diagnose and self-treat the colds and viruses your children bring home from school, and relegate your doctor to an occasional call when you find that your crying child has a high fever that cannot be controlled by aspirin, or when you think your blood pressure should be checked. Even that can now be done at home with a do-it-yourself blood pressure kit. Neither you nor your doctor has much opportunity to practice "empathy" anymore; little wonder you are able and willing to sue when things don't seem to go right. And little wonder you have become just another chart or billing card in a physician's office files. Your fault? Your doctor's fault? I think both patient and doctor share the blame.

WERE YOU FULLY INFORMED?

In this enlightened age, with our heightened awareness of the rights of individuals, were you angry because your doctor did not fully prepare you for possible unsatisfactory results or uncomfortable side effects resulting from your treatment? A 1979 malpractice suit led to a judgment against a physician for having failed to warn a fortyish expectant mother that the chances of her giving birth to a child with Down's syndrome (mongolism) were high because of her age. Had the doctor told her, the suit alleged, she would have elected to have an abortion. The court ruled that the physician had been negligent in not fully *informing* the patient, and was therefore liable for the costs of caring for and rearing the child.

In today's society, the patient has the moral and the legal right to be the final judge of all treatment to be administered, and all acts carried out on his or her body, and for refusal to accept any or all of them. This is probably quite justified, though as a physician I sometimes doubt that the patient is sufficiently knowledgeable about medicine always to render this judgment competently. Nevertheless, the patient should certainly have the right to refuse treatments that are not desired, or to choose between treatment options when, for example, one carries both a higher incidence of side effects and a better chance of success. The physician in the Down's syndrome case was found guilty not only for his failure to fully inform his patient, but for not having offered her the opportunity to submit to amniocentesis, the withdrawal of a small sample of fluid from the sac surrounding the fetus which is submitted to microscopic examination for possible identification of the chromosomal aberrations that are characteristic of Down's syndrome. Had she had amniocentesis, the woman could have known in advance that her unborn child was, indeed, mongoloid, and could have chosen (or not chosen—we will never know) to abort the pregnancy. Such is the fine degree to which the patient's right to be informed has been defined.

Informed consent is the term commonly applied to the disclosure of "all" information to the patient. Those simple forms that were once signed by every patient upon admission to a hospital, stating, "I consent to have Dr. ————— or any person he/she may designate perform such tests or treatments on me as deemed necessary," are now little more than a source of humor. "As deemed necessary" indeed! The doctrine of *informed* consent now requires that the doctor reveal all possible adverse or undesirable effects of a *proposed* treatment, and that the patient consent to the procedure only after having been so informed. Even today, it may be difficult to refuse to sign such blanket consent statements as are shoved under your nose, by the officious and rarely friendly hospital admissions clerk, but the form is irrelevant. Signed or not, the blanket consent forms are meaningless in today's legal environment.

On the other hand, if you have been properly informed of the risks inherent in a medical or surgical procedure (for example, the chances of death in the operating room or in the immediate postoperative period from open-heart surgery), and you have willingly accepted the risk, the doctor, in the absence of sheer negligence, is fairly well protected should anything go wrong. This does not, of course, apply if your death or adverse reaction comes about as a result of a failure to take certain steps that are considered necessary to counteract emergency situations that develop in the course of the operation. Once again, each member of the operating team—the surgeon, assistants, anesthesiologist, and nurses—is held to a standard of care consistent with each one's training and education.

Doctors can under certain circumstances be held liable for their partners' acts of negligence, and even for acts of their assistants or nonmedical employees. If you call your doctor to request assistance in an emergency, but the secretary refuses to put you through because the doctor is "busy with a patient," or it is not the "telephone hour" and the secretary fails to appreciate the urgency of the situation, the doctor may be held liable for untoward events that occur as a result. It is immaterial whether this was general policy or whether the secretary alone decided without authorization to be protective of your doctor's schedule. A doctor cannot make amends by calling back three hours later after office hours are over if the patient expired in the meantime!

It must be understood, though, that a general surgeon in a rural area who atempts open-heart surgery is held to the standards of an open-heart-surgery team in a major medical center known for its skill and experience in performing such procedures. Once your surgeon has *represented* himself as having the required degree of competence and skill, he is held to the standard of like physicians. He cannot deny negligence on the basis of not having been fully trained in the special techniques needed. This defense is paramount to having committed a fraud on his patient by claiming to be competent in the first place.

Did your doctor "assure" you that the lump in your breast is "probably benign," only to proceed immediately to perform a radical mastectomy after receiving the pathologist's report that the lump was malignant? No informed consent here, to be sure. Because of the implications affecting your physical and psychological well-being, your feminine image, and your sexuality, before the biopsy most physicians will present a formal statement describing the degree of uncertainty of their manual breast examination, the results of mammography, thermography, or xerography tests, the need for biopsy to determine malignancy definitely, and their plans if the lump should turn out to be cancer. It is customary to have not only the patient, but also the husband or next of kin, sign such statements, and patients can ask for time after the biopsy to consider the alternatives.

If you are faced with the possibility of a radical mastectomy, and aren't sure that's the option you prefer, *Don't Sign*. If your surgeon becomes indignant and refuses to go ahead with the biopsy unless he or she has blanket permission to do a radical mastectomy as well, don't sulk. Get another surgeon more receptive to your beliefs. Or do you *want* the doctor to play Daddy and make your decision for you? It's a perfectly normal feeling, but unless you say so, your doctor can't know. Only you can know.

Many doctors have difficulty telling some patients the entire truth about their conditions, the unfavorable outcomes expected, and every side effect of treatment that could possibly occur. When the diagnosis is unquestionably a hopeless, fatal illness, or a permanently or seriously disabling one, some patients can take such news very well, while others are not emotionally prepared to handle it. There are probably fewer of the latter type than most doctors believe, but the belief is widespread and does influence the manner in which the doctor handles the situation. Some patients are mildly neurotic or hypochondriacal, and will experience every possible side effect mentioned by the doctor. I have conducted research trials of a new antihistamine drug in which the patients receiving the placebo —the inactive lookalike given to some of the patients to validate the results and control the experiment—experienced drowsiness to almost the same extent as the patients receiving the medication! All had hay fever, had been taking antihistamines for years, and "knew" that drowsiness is a common side effect. In other clinical trials with diet pills, the incidence of insomnia, nervousness, and irritability was quite high among the placebo patients. Again, these were people who had taken other diet medications in the past, and who "knew" that such side effects usually occurred. The power of suggestion is very great, and placebos or "sugar pills" can also effect a surprising degree of relief of symptoms, especially if administered by a sympathetic doctor.

Is withholding information ever justified? A good rule is to consider whether the deception is for the benefit of the physician or the patient. Often, the attempts to withhold information about impending death are inconsequential. Families and physicians may engage in elaborate games to keep terminally ill patients from finding out, but most of these patients do know the truth. Not infrequently, the patients are keeping their knowledge to themselves in a similar attempt to spare the feelings of relatives or even a highly respected doctor.

At one time, treating a patient (performing an unexpected operation like the radical mastectomy, for example) without the specific consent of the patient or parent (if a minor) or legal guardian, was considered assault. The current trend, however, in accordance with today's thinking on the subject of informed consent, generally considers lack of informed consent to be *malpractice*, and the courts treat it as such.

WHEN YOUR DOCTOR WON'T LISTEN

In this age of enlightenment, you may at times preform opinions about the eventual diagnosis your doctor will make, or even suggest preferred forms of treatment, perhaps based on information (accurate or not) you obtained from a recent magazine article or TV show. Sometimes such suggestions are highly valid, based on your detailed understanding of your own condition, habits, bodily needs, and past experiences to which your doctor does not yet have access. It is, regrettably, extremely difficult for most physicians to accept suggestions from patients. Such suggestions appear as direct attacks on the doctor's integrity and competence. I have known physicians to continue to defend their own choice of treatment long after having been proven wrong through hindsight, or when advised by colleagues that the treatment was inadequate or incorrect. After all, even doctors are people, subject to the weaknesses, errors, and pride of all beings, though the nature of their profession may make it difficult for them to accept this basic fact.

The doctor's lifelong war against sickness and death, and his frequent victories, tend to create a feeling of being just a bit superhuman, what I have for years termed a "Deity Complex." It is this Deity Complex that compels an otherwise sensible physician to drive at ninety miles per hour down an icy highway answering an emergency call ("I am out doing the Lord's work, therefore nothing can happen to me"), and also to reject as meaningless nonsense all ideas, concepts, and suggestions about the diagnosis and treatment of sickness that do not originate with him, or at least with other members of the profession.

In moments of deep reflection, it has occurred to me that this Deity Complex may be necessary for the practice of the profession. If a doctor does not feel capable of conquering the Angel of Death, why institute any treatment at all? A doctor cannot be a fatalist ("What will be, will be"; "When my time comes or when the Lord calls me, I'll go"), for to believe this is to admit the total futility of any efforts to cure. But like all complexes, this one, too, can be carried to excess. If your suggestion is ridiculed or ignored, and the doctor is later shown to have been right, you should quickly forget about it. If, on the other hand, your doctor turns out to have been wrong, and by some strange coincidence, it appears that *your* idea was better, then you have one more reason or justification for a malpractice suit. But the next time such a situation comes up in your dealings with your doctor, recall *why* he acts in this manner. With patience and understanding on both sides comes a better relationship, whether the combatants be nations, spouses, parents and children, or doctors and patients. Will a malpractice suit make things right? Were you really injured by your doctor's seeming arrogance, or just offended? Must empathy come only from the doctor?

Sometimes it is your doctor's choice of language rather than the information or lack thereof that he or she metes out that stimulates the resentment and paves the road for a lawsuit. If a doctor attempts to gain your agreement to a proposed treatment by a choice of words deliberately intended to frighten you ("You are going to bleed to death!" instead of "You will probably experience some additional bleeding or spotting"), this is an improper exercise of his role as the expert medical practitioner, and an abuse of the Deity Complex.

THE TRUE VICTIM OF NEGLIGENCE AND INCOMPETENCE

There are certainly a significant number of patients who, having placed their faith and trust in their physicians, have been the victims of inadequate or incompetent management. A minority of all such cases taken up with lawyers is unquestionably justified. Some plaintiffs fully deserve judgments in their favor, and deserve compensation for having been injured through wrongful acts.

The first set of laws that dealt with social rules and included some very specific regulations about the practice of medicine was assembled and inscribed in stone about four thousand years ago. It is known as the Code of Hammurabi, and the original is on display at the Louvre in Paris.

The Code of Hammurabi describes the payment due a physician for various services, and *the penalty for certain acts that today we call malpractice*. Comparison of the fees and the penalties for failure does make one wonder why anyone practiced the healing arts in ancient Babylonia:

> If a doctor has treated a Free Man with a metal knife for a severe wound, and has cured the Free Man . . . then he shall receive ten shekels of silver.

> If a doctor has treated a man with a metal knife for a severe wound, and has caused the man to die . . . his hands shall be cut off.

The first recorded malpractice suit in the United States was filed against Dr. Samuel Guthery of Stafford, Connecticut, in 1793 for incompetent and cruel amputation of a breast that resulted in the death of the woman. Dr. Guthery lost the case, and paid compensatory damages.[1]

Redress for wrongful acts, and universal access to the courts, are inherent in the Anglo-American system of justice, and stem back many centuries to the establishment of the King's Chancery Courts in England. Judicial officers appointed by the sovereign traveled throughout the realm, setting up court wherever requested, hearing complaints of alleged wrongdoing by the citizenry in a rather informal manner, and adjudicating them in the name of the King

[1] J. Nemec (ed.), *Highlights in Medicolegal Relations*. Prepared for the Dept. of Health, Education and Welfare. (Washington, D.C.: U.S. Government Printing Office, 1976), 69.

as they thought fit. When direct restitution of a loss was not possible, monetary compensation was considered a fair substitute.

Inasmuch as the medical profession expects, even demands, almost total faith from its patients, and since a doctor does at times literally take a patient's life into his own hands, the patient who is injured as a result of the doctor's incompetence or negligence, whose faith has been compromised, is entitled to compensation.

A life, once lost, cannot be regained. And health, if irrevocably compromised, cannot be recovered. The common form of restitution, therefore, is financial, however inadequate it may be in replacing the loss. Our legal system and our society nevertheless recognize it as just compensation.

Certain types of injuries are so obvious as to require only the barest minimum of a trial sufficient to establish the facts. The law says that in such cases "the fact speaks for itself" (*res ipsa loquitur*). In other words, the act complained of *could not have occurred unless the physician was negligent.* An example of this type of lawsuit is that in which an instrument has been left inside the body of a patient during surgery. There is no reason known to medical science for doing so; the wrongful act is obvious, and could not have occurred without the doctor's negligence. No further proof is needed other than to establish this and two additional facts, and the only defense possible would be to prove that the instrument was not in the body after the operation mentioned in the lawsuit, but rather the incident occurred during a later operation and the wrong doctor is being sued.

The two additional elements that are necessary to make a clear case on the basis of this doctrine are:

1. The "agent" (object) that was the cause of the injury was under the exclusive control of the alleged wrongdoer, i.e., the doctor being sued.

2. The injury was not caused by or contributed to by the patient.

Most allegations of malpractice are not, however, that simple and clear-cut. They must be proven, and what must be shown is not only that the treatment was unsuccessful, but that the doctor did not practice his or her profession at the level of physicians of similar education and training, and *because* of this, the outcome was less than favorable.

Patients should feel no guilt connected with such a law-suit. The only guilt should be that felt by the doctor who knowingly committed the negligence, or who gave less than his best to his patient. Despite popular opinion to the contrary, few things anger doctors more than a clear case of negligence on the part of a colleague. It reflects on all of us. In fact, such strong feelings on the part of doctors, such consuming pride in their professional standards, are the patients' greatest protection against negligence. No doctor *wants* to be negligent, and only a few are so callous as not to care if they are. The problems arise after the doctor is confronted with his or her negligence. No profession engages in more behind-the-scenes self-policing than the medical profession, and though they are usually reluctant to talk about it, doctors will take firm steps to penalize a colleague who is obviously incompetent. Such punishments usually come to the attention of the public only when the incompetent doctor files suit for a court's reversal of the penalties levied by his or her colleagues, such as revoking the privileges to practice in a given hospital.

How do you know if you have been the victim of malpractice? Competent attorneys knowledgeable in this field of law will submit the allegations to medical consultants who will review the case impartially, and give an opinion on the case's merit. The diligent attorney takes on and files only those suits for which there is good reason to believe that the patient's complaint of wrongful acts will be proven justified. An attorney will not invest time and money in a case that has little chance of success, though "merit" and "chances of success" are apparently not equated in the lawyers' minds. (A recent nationwide survey concluded that while 90 percent of the lawyers interviewed would not pursue a case if the medical evaluation seemed to indicate the absence of negligence, the criteria by which they reached this evaluation were not at all clear.) Still, attorneys who defend doctors in malpractice cases are highly experienced in this type of case, for they are usually the attorneys employed by or routinely retained by the insurance carrier. The plaintiff's counsel, the lawyer who represents the patient, would therefore rather not go to court with a very weak case, for he or she stands to lose not only the investment of time and money in exchange for little or no fee, but may also experience some decrease in his professional reputation. Chapter 5 will discuss the procedures for selecting and cooperating with an attorney for the preparation and processing of the lawsuit.

If you have strong doubts about the situation, one source of guidance is first to file a complaint with, and request a review by, the local county medical society. Almost all such professional groups have a malpractice review committee, sometimes jointly with the county bar association, which will hear the details of the case and advise the patient if it appears that malpractice may have been committed. Occasionally, the case is heard without the identity of the physician being made known to the committee. In some parts of the country, two adjoining county societies will review each other's patient complaints. In each case, every attempt is made to render an impartial, purely medical opinion on the merits of the complaint. This does not result in any obligation on the part of the patient, who may still elect to file suit or not as he or she chooses. These committees are by no means an attempt by the medical profession to stop lawsuits. Rather, they are widely lauded by attorneys and judges for their serious efforts to ensure justice for the truly wronged patients by heading off the frivolous cases that clog the court calendar.

OTHER CATEGORIES OF PLAINTIFFS

We all know that some people are "suit happy." They sue everyone about everything. Their conversation at cocktail parties is full of lurid tales of who they have just sued and who they are about to sue. Their first thought, and often their first act, after a real or imagined wrong or slight from a merchant, a service person, even a neighbor, is to call or visit their lawyer. Many of these calls do lead to a lawsuit, some won, some lost, but all provide some inner satisfaction to the complainant and income to the attorney. These people are the lawyer's equivalent of the doctor's hypochondriacal patient, that time-consuming and rather frustrating individual who imagines a serious disease behind every sensation or twinge of discomfort. There is almost nothing that can be done to discourage such people. Their suits prevail in court just often enough to continue to feed their belief that litigation is justified.

Medical doctors usually earn well above the national average at any stage of their career after their training period is completed, and as a result, they become objects of envy to those who do not subscribe to the Tenth Commandment's "Thou shalt not covet. . . ." A few patients believe that any performance by their doctor that falls short of perfection represents a substantive basis for redistributing his or her wealth, preferably in the patient's direction. Such patients are similar to the "suit happy" people, but their goal is more specific: they want *money*, rationalizing to themselves that the doctor is well enough off that a "small loss" will not seriously interfere with his or her style of living, and the insurance company will probably pay most or all of it anyway. There is malice in this way of thinking, however, and such persons should not be encouraged unless they have a valid cause to sue. There are many incidents wherein the presiding judge at a trial or pretrial hearing has declared that the plaintiff's case has little substance, but that the doctor or the insurance company should "give them a few thousand dollars just to end the matter." Since the "few thousand dollars" is inevitably less than the cost of continuing litigation, it is paid, and the blackmail has succeeded. These are called "nuisance suits," and should be vigorously discouraged.

Finally, we come to a most unusual form of plaintiff. This is a patient who has either become extraordinarily dependent on the doctor psychologically, or has suggested or fantasized a romantic or sexual entanglement with him. Common to both, however, is the doctor's real or imagined *rejection* of the patient. Rarely does the doctor desire or even perceive such a relationship with a patient, and may consciously or unconsciously appear to be "rejecting" the individual. Some patients react to this "rejection" with anger, neurosis, depression, even suicide. Some seek revenge, and a lawsuit is a perfectly legal vendetta, free of the risks, inconveniences, and disastrous consequences of more violent forms of revenge.

Have you recognized yourself in this discussion? More than likely, you still feel your proposed malpractice suit is justified, that you belong to the group of patients who have truly been victims of negligence. Now identify your doctor in the next chapter—if you can.

CHAPTER 3

WHO GETS SUED, AND WHY?

THE DOCTOR WHO IS TOO BUSY TO TALK

The average work week for a doctor in a one-physician private practice is about sixty hours long. For doctors gathered together in group practices with one or more other physicians in the same specialty, it is closer to forty-five or fifty hours long.

When you recall the times you tried to reach your doctor but could not, and waited hours, or even until the next day, for him to call you back, you might think those figures somewhat on the incredible side, or even come up with a far less polite comment! But the doctor's "work week" extends far beyond the hours spent in the office seeing patients. Other time-consuming duties include daily hospital rounds (1–3 hours); possibly supervising interns and residents—and teaching medical students as well if the hospital is affiliated with a medical school; attendance at one or more hospital staff and committee meetings, which are mandatory if the doctor is to retain admission privileges and a staff appointment; completion of hospital charts and records according to the standards of the Joint Commission on Accreditation of Hospitals; completion of or at least dictation of the information for Blue Cross, Blue Shield, Medicare, worker's compensation, and private insurance claim forms; and possibly supervision of hospital outpatient clinics. In addition, your doctor may also make extra visits to the hospital if a patient is in critical condition, has taken a turn for the worse, or is in the immediate postoperative period. He or she may be called in for an urgent consultation by another physician. Even the time your doctor spends reading medical journals and textbooks or attending postgraduate educational lectures and seminars (what you call "conventions") are duties that cannot be shirked, for the accumulation of continuing-education hours is not only essential for the proper performance of the profession, but is mandatory in many states for retention of a medical license. In certain instances, a minimum number of such credits per year is required for maintenance of the specialty certification for which the doctor is reexamined periodically. In my practice days, my work week averaged closer to seventy hours, but I belonged to the waning years of the house-call era!

These heavy demands on their time make some doctors reluctant to take the extra minutes to talk at any length with their patients, explaining fully what is wrong, and what can be done about it, and answering questions. Dr. Marcus Welby could spend as much time as necessary on every patient; he only saw one patient per week (per episode, that is!).

All of this, however, is an explanation—not a justification, for there is none—for a doctor's failure to inform a patient completely. It is part of your doctor's moral as well as legal duty to ensure that you understand your condition, and time-consuming or not, a full explanation is just as important to the relationship as the history-taking or the examination. Failure to communicate with the patient, or failure to *inform* the patient, is frequently the foundation upon which future dissatisfactions and lawsuits are built. If *your* doctor is too busy to talk to you, find one who is not. "Busy-ness" is no measure of the quality, the competence, or the reputation of the doctor; some of the greatest men of medicine, past and present, were particularly noted for their close relationship with their patients. Remember that word empathy!

THE DOCTOR WHO IS TOO BUSY TO LISTEN

This is not the same doctor as the previous one. This doctor's problem is not necessarily a busy schedule, but an exaggerated sense of his own importance. And a diminished sense of yours.

It is characteristic of societies that employ house servants, or in other centuries slaves, that the masters felt no restraint about discussing any subject while the servants were in the room going about their duties. These individuals were considered "nonpersons," no ones, and no importance was given to their presence. If they dared to enter the conversation they were banished, or worse.

Patients are a kind of nonperson to the Doctor Who Is Too Busy To Listen. You may be in the doctor's presence and asking questions, but this doctor heareth not. Such a physician cannot accept the fact that you might have something to contribute to the discussion of your illness other than the specific answers to the specific questions *he* or *she* asked.

This doctor, enamored of the sound of his own voice but deaf to the sound of others, also earns a place on the list of likely malpractice defendants. The doctor has *angered* the patient by that indifference to his remarks, and has set the stage for a lawsuit at some future time when a treatment falls short of expectations. The patient whose doctor *has* listened, conversely, feels as if they have failed together, that they are a team, and must simply make a second and better effort to effect a cure or improvement. This patient feels that he or she has been *participating* in the relationship. Empathy again!

THE DOCTOR WHO IS DROWNING IN A DEITY COMPLEX

This good soul *wants* to listen to you, and may even appear to be doing so, but like the Doctor Who Is Too Busy To Listen, is so totally convinced that he alone is the sole source of useful information about your condition that his ears no longer seem to hear a patient's voice. This doctor's place in the Hall of Infamy results from listening to you without hearing you. Or perhaps this doctor hears you without listening to you. Either way, he or she has earned a priority place on the malpractice waiting list.

As I mentioned earlier, while the doctor's Deity Complex or inflated ego may be necessary to preserve his sanity in a profession surrounded by suffering and death, it must exist in moderation, tempered by the kind of empathy and feeling toward patients that once made the doctor the most beloved of professional servants. We will permit this complex so long as the doctor demonstrates feelings for the patients and convinces them of true *participation* in their suffering, and does not view medicine as only a means of earning a living or as an activity to be engaged in for monetary reasons between golf games.

More doctors appear to belong to this group than really do. Beneath the surface, the majority of doctors do care, though *on* the surface many seem to have lost the ability to communicate this fact.

Sometimes, a breakdown or failure of adequate communication between the referring doctor and the specialist consultant appears to cause the lawsuit. In such situations, the seed of thought about negligence is planted in the patient's mind by the specialist who has failed to understand or inform himself or herself about, or chooses to ignore, the depth and diligence of the efforts at diagnosis and treatment that had been made by the primary physician. With the habit of downgrading the performance and competence of the Family Physician that is so prevalent among specialists, the specialist implies that the patient has been injured or wronged when, in fact, a more thorough investigation of the facts would have avoided any such unwarranted conclusions and accusations. Such a specialist is essentially drowning in a private Deity Complex. It is a fact, however, that the greatest source of malpractice cases is patients who have heard criticism from their specialist or current doctor of their previous doctor's work. The criticism may be just or not, but it gives the patient the idea of suing.

THE INCOMPETENT DOCTOR

There are some doctors who consider that the objective of attending medical school is to pass the final exams, receive the diploma, and obtain a license. Having accomplished these goals, such doctors close and seal their minds to additional or advancing medical knowledge as effectively as the priests of ancient Egypt sealed King Tut's tomb. They will rarely assimilate a new bit of information or knowledge for the rest of their lives, and they become increasingly incompetent as they fall farther and farther behind in the galloping world of medical science.

As in any profession, there are a few individuals who become licensed but who probably should never have been allowed to do so. A minimum of knowledge and a good "line" carries them for many years, sometimes a lifetime, to the detriment of some of their patients. And every few years, there are stories of people who learn the "lingo" and succeed in masquerading as physicians without having ever attended medical school. They sometimes get away with it for an unbelievable period of time. A little blarney goes a long way, even in medicine.

Any geographical group of physicians contains a small percentage of unfortunate doctors who have become victims of mental illness, or succumbed to alcoholism or drug addiction. While fundamentally not incompetent, their *performance* under such conditions is inevitably inadequate. Even more unfortunate is the fact that their colleagues often protect them and cover up for them. They understand that these doctors are ill rather than incompetent, and they want to "help" them. Perhaps there is also a touch of "there, but for the grace of God, go I." The sympathy is misplaced, however, for such doctors are a menace to their patients, their colleagues, their families, and themselves. They do not deserve punishment, but they do need to be removed from patient-care responsibilities until they are once again capable of functioning in a responsible manner. Sometimes only a lawsuit, usually with adequate justification, stops such doctors from practicing.

Still other doctors, excellent physicians in their prime, continue to practice to an age when they are functioning far below their earlier standards, below even what is considered minimal competence. Firmly established in the community and the hospital hierarchy with a long tradition of faithful service, such doctors go on because their colleagues are reluctant to take any action against them. Their practices are their own, and short of revoking their licenses, no one can stop them from seeing patients so long as there are patients willing to visit. But declining vision, failing memory, and unsteady hands have no place in medical practice. Loyalty and gratitude for past services can be expressed in other, safer ways. Who needs a surgeon who because of shaking hands or poor vision cuts or clamps anything within two inches of the spot he aimed for? It would be kind to help such a doctor relinquish duties and responsibilities with dignity, far kinder than to have the doctor suffer a devastating malpractice suit. An attorney remarked to me once that in his opinion, there should be a mandatory retirement age of fifty-five for doctors. I could not agree with that, however. Were it ever to come true, we might be spared the senile efforts of a few doctors, but would also lose the great wisdom of so many superb leaders of medicine who continue to give us the benefit of their unparalleled experience for many years, even decades, after that arbitrary age.

Many medical societies maintain committees, often called Committees on Impaired Physicians or some similar name, for the express purpose of helping those unfortunate doctors who, the medical society is the first to admit, "often do not recognize their health problems." They endeavor to help impaired doctors seek proper treatment, and at times will engage in a bit of arm twisting to pressure the impaired physician into a temporary period of practice suspension. They warn that family, friends, and associates of these unfortunate doctors should avoid misguided sympathy, which only enables the condition to deteriorate further. Unspoken, but clearly implied, is that the patients of such doctors are in serious jeopardy.

The medical profession also contains its portion of out-and-out incompetents who know they are, and have always been incompetent, and don't seem to care. The patient who brings one of these doctors into court to answer for his or her actions may be doing a great service to society. Often it is the only way the incompetent's colleagues can take disciplinary measures. Occasionally the information brought out in the trial results in revocation of this doctor's license by state authorities. License revocation is a drastic action to take, but such careers are better ended.

THE DOCTOR WHO CAN'T REMEMBER

Many malpractice suits are based on the doctor's failure to give adequate follow-up instructions; to recall the advice given or the medication prescribed last week; or to remember to question you about, or refer to his chart regarding your drug allergies, previous reactions, previous drug resistance, or other such mitigating factors that might have otherwise suggested different advice or instructions. Some doctors don't even recall talking to a patient the previous day. While it is certainly not difficult to forget a conversation held at three in the morning while half asleep, doctors should make some effort to jot down such information for reference the next morning.

When such a case reaches the courtroom it is one of the most difficult to try. Two conflicting versions of the occurrence, of the instructions, the advice, and so on, are given, both probably with sincerity. Humans are noted for poor recollection of details, which grows ever poorer with time. When a malpractice case finally comes to trial *several years* after the incident took place, the memory of both defendant and plaintiff has grown hazy, and has had subjective feelings and wishful thinking superimposed on it. It is often impossible to determine who (if either) is recounting an accurate story of what happened. The court must then rely entirely on the testimony of witnesses, if there were any, who can confirm one version of the story or the other.

If the controversial conversation or consultation did indeed take place in the wee hours of the morning or on Sunday, the doctor's only witness is likely to be his wife. Even with the best of intentions, she can hardly be considered an impartial objective witness. But who is *your* witness? *Your* wife or husband? He or she is no better than the doctor's witness, to be sure. If a pharmacist becomes involved in the situation along the way, this might be helpful. He is not only a somewhat impartial third party, but is also supposed to keep accurate records, especially the details of all telephone conversations with doctors. If you have such a witness, all to the good; he may succeed in settling the controversy. If not, you must depend solely on your attorney to convince a judge and/or jury that your version is true and the doctor's is false.

The message here, of course, is to *keep records*. Even a slip of note paper that records the day, date, time, and a brief summary of your conversation with the doctor can be helpful. A bound notebook in which this entry is made in chronological order with other such telephone notations is much better. The notebook needn't record only medical matters. How about also writing down such things as the time or times you called the contractor about the unfinished job in your basement, or how often you called a credit card company about the error on your bill? A bound book is the most credible record because entries cannot be "stuck in" at a later date. Books of this nature are kept by inventors, and can be the sole basis on which a patent is granted to one inventor and not another because one has recorded an earlier notation of a discovery. If keeping accurate records helps your doctor and druggist, why not adopt the technique to help yourself?

The doctor who doesn't remember specifics, and doesn't keep complete records, has an open invitation to malpractice suits.

WHEN THE DOCTOR IS THE VICTIM

In the preceding chapter, I identified several types of individuals who sue doctors for reasons quite unrelated to competence, or to the actual occurrence of negligence or a wrongful act. It is only fair to include the doctor as victim, principally so that you may know that just because you hear that your doctor, or some other doctor, has been sued, you are not justified in concluding that he is necessarily negligent, incompetent, egotistical, overly busy, careless, or any of the other characteristics of defendants that I have discussed. Every plaintiff who sues in the absence of a real negligent or incompetent act has victimized a doctor. Such a plaintiff may have caused the doctor financial loss, loss of prestige, loss of self-esteem, and anguish—or worse. This subject is explored more thoroughly in Chapter 7.

While this chapter about defendant doctors may appear somewhat shorter than the preceding one, which discussed plantiff patients, it is certainly not because I favor the doctor over the patient. It is simply easier to identify and spotlight the kinds of doctors who are the defendants in most malpractice suits than it is to pinpoint the many reasons that lead a patient to sue. But what about the other side of the coin? What about the doctor who almost never gets sued? What is *he* like? It has been my observation through the years that such doctors probably fit the following description rather closely:

> They have a close relationship with their patients.
> They have a deep sense of empathy and kindness toward the sick.
> They earn just as much as other doctors, but don't appear to flaunt wealth or to give the impression that money is their prime motive for practicing medicine (even if it really is!).
> They treat the patients as equals, and explain their actions to the patients when they feel it is necessary to insist, for sound scientific reasons, on a particular form of treatment.
> They are up to date in medical knowledge.
> They call for consultations when appropriate.
> They keep careful and complete records of all dealings with the patients.
> They are lucky.

CHAPTER 4

WITH THE CONSENT OF THE PATIENT

WHY YOU ARE ASKED TO GRANT CONSENT

There was a time not so very long ago when the authority image of the physician was considered indisputable and unquestionable. We experienced a symptom or collection of symptoms. We visited the doctor with some fear and trepidation and subjected ourselves to whatever examinations, tests, discomforts, and indignities the doctor suggested, with scarcely a thought or doubt about their necessity. After all, why on earth would the doctor do such things if they were not necessary for our own benefit, either to permit a correct diagnosis of the problem or to select what, in our doctor's opinion, was the best treatment for the condition or for relief of the symptoms? When a patient was admitted to a hospital, he or she was presented with a paper and instructed to sign. This form gave blanket permission to the doctor or any designated assistants or substitutes to do whatever was thought necessary for the patient's benefit. Few patients objected, for it was either presented at the time of admission when anxiety was overwhelming, or shortly before surgery when the senses were already partially dulled by sedatives. The alternative to signing the form, the patient was quickly informed by a clerk or nurse, was quite simply that neither the doctor nor the hospital could do anything to help the patient.

Such unilateral decision making is no longer tolerated in the world of doctor–patient relationships, and I dare say that it is not terribly missed (except by a few doctors). Today, the public—the consumer, patient, or whatever— is more knowledgeable about many things, including medical care, and demands to know what is to be done to him or her and *why*. If we concede the changing attitudes toward consumer awareness and the right to determine one's own destiny, then the sick or injured patient also has a right to have a say in what the doctor proposes to do. In cases where several alternative treatments are available, the patient should demand the right to be advised about each of them and to know why the physician has chosen any particular one, and rejected the others. (For example, he is more familiar with this one, for better or for worse; the "other" ones are new and untested; the patient's condition or coexistent diseases may form a barrier to successful or safe treatment with one of the rejected therapies; and so on.)

Whether adequate to the task or not, the patient demands participation in the decision-making process and reserves the right to listen to the doctor's thought processes and make the final decision. This has come to be known as the Doctrine of Informed Consent, where the key word is "informed." It is a very new concept, generally considered to have originated as a firm principle of law only in 1960 when a Kansas judge rendered a decision in the case of Natanson *v*. Kline (350 P 2d 1093, Kans 1960):

> A man is the master of his own body and he may expressly prohibit the performance of life-saving surgery or other medical treatment. A doctor may well believe that an operation or other form of treatment is desirable or necessary, but the law does not permit him to substitute his own judgment for that of the patient by any form of artifice or deception.

In other words, the right to choose or refuse medical treatment is as fundamental to the late twentieth-century American concept of freedom as the right to choose or reject representatives to government—and the citizen/patient often makes his or her decision with the same reckless abandon in the one case as in the other. Be that as it may, this decision was the first strong pronouncement by a court, though the basic concept was enunciated way back in 1914 by Judge Benjamin Cardozo, later a Justice of the Supreme Court, in Schloendorff *v*. Society of NY Hosp. (211 N.Y. 125, 129–30, 105 N.E. 92, 1914). He wrote:

> Every human being of adult years and sound mind has a right to determine what shall be done with his own body and a surgeon who performs an operation without his patient's consent commits an assault for which he is liable in damages.

What have we, then? Basically, the principle of informed consent means that the doctor proposing some treatment or procedure to a patient must give the patient sufficient information about the proposal, how likely it is to be successful, what risks are involved, what side effects or discomfort may be produced, what alternatives are available, why the procedure chosen is, in the doctor's opinion, the best for this patient and why the others were rejected, and what the risks of *no* treatment are, such that a patient of reasonable intelligence and average education may understand and be able to make a reasonably intelligent decision, being as objective as anyone can be in such a situation. The patient should, therefore, be in a position to agree or disagree with the doctor on some better basis than a good relationship with the doctor or blind faith in the physician's healing powers, or conversely, a decided distrust of all members of the medical profession and anything they may advise or suggest. Even today, some patients, particularly if they are poorly educated, immigrants, or (especially) if they are elderly and/or very ill, can succumb to the authority of a strong-willed, egotistical, or pontificating physician and "consent" to things they would rather not have done to them. There are, as there always are, occasional examples of utterly disgraceful deception on the part of doctors, but they are not common. Today, doctors are more likely to err in the opposite direction, on the side of ultraconservatism, but more on that later.

The case most often cited as the classic example of a physician's taking advantage of a patient to gain consent when he otherwise could not is a 1955 Nevada case, Corn *v.* French (289 P 2d 173, Nev 1955). The surgeon obtained "informed consent" from his patient to perform a "mastectomy," aware that she did not know the meaning of the medical term, by assuring her that he had no intention of removing her breast! She signed but later sued, and you do not have to be a professor of law to guess how the decision went at the trial.

It is even considered improper in this enlightened world of ours for a doctor to carry that old-fashioned idea of bedside manner or "TLC" to the point of assuring a patient before surgery that "there is no danger; everything will be just fine," when, in fact, *any* operation carries with it a certain element of risk. Such pronouncements are no longer viewed as the kind words of an empathetic physician, but as a legally binding assurance or warranty that is untrue, and a negating of the precept of *informed* consent.

What a dilemma this has become for the sincere doctor who truly wishes to do what is legally correct *and* what is best for a patient, all the more so when the two objectives no longer coincide. How much to tell? How much is "enough" and when does it become "too much"? When is it "overkill"? There are as yet no clear answers to these questions, for the subject remains a hotly debated and highly controversial one within the medical profession, between the medical profession and the legal profession, between both professions and the consumer advocates, and between everyone and the government.

THE SERIOUS VERSUS THE INCONSEQUENTIAL

Extremes are rarely the route of choice or preference, or even desirable. It is good for your doctor to reveal to you how successful, in his or her experience and the combined experience of the medical profession as reported in the medical journals and textbooks, a particular proposed course of therapy is likely to be. Of course, your doctor will speak of "averages" or statistical probability, all of which bears only a somewhat small relation to what will happen to *you*. The fact that only four cases of every hundred do not survive a certain surgical procedure allows your doctor to state that statistically you have ninety-six chances out of a hundred to come through it alive, but in no way permits the physician to state categorically that you will be part of the group of ninety-six who survive and not one of the four who do not—any more than knowing the odds at a Las Vegas slot machine permits you to predict which pull of the handle will win you the jackpot.

By the same reasoning, it is *not* good for your doctor

to tell you every single adverse experience or bad reaction that has ever been reported in a patient taking the medication prescribed. Some of these have been reported only once or twice out of millions of doses administered, and even then the side effects may not necessarily have been the *result* of the medication. All that is known, and by Food and Drug Administration (FDA) regulation included in the official information about a drug, is that some of these reactions just happened to occur while the patient was taking the medication.

Persons who are ill and perhaps frightened have enough emotional turmoil with which to deal and do not really need such additional information of questionable value. Few patients are sufficiently familiar with the manner of reporting medical information to be able to place such information *in context* and *in perspective*. In the interest of scientific completeness, aided somewhat by government regulations about "full disclosure," it is the common practice in the health sciences to report with seemingly equal weight the *common* side effects of a drug, those experienced by significant numbers of the persons taking the medicine, and those occasionally or rarely seen. Likewise the law requires the disclosure of reactions known to be a result of the medication as well as those for which there is only a casual (not a "causal") relationship of time, i.e., the reaction occurred during the same period in which this medication was being administered, but no direct cause-and-effect relationship has ever been clearly established.

There are those among us who handle bad news better than others. Some people prefer to be told when death seems inevitable so they can put their affairs in order, say their "good-byes," make amends with estranged friends or relatives, or make peace with their Creator. Others would rather remain in ignorance until the moment arrives, and be left to pass peacefully into eternity. As I mentioned earlier, among the more ludicrous absurdities of medical practice, familiar to every physician, is when family and doctor do everything to protect the patient from knowledge of impending death, while the patient, well aware of the situation, feigns ignorance in order to spare relatives the emotional suffering of having to talk about it with him. All of them wish it were otherwise, and not infrequently, the survivors suffer pangs of guilt for years afterward, having been "denied" the opportunity to express love, patch up old quarrels, or otherwise bid the departing one a loving farewell. Physicians are the worst of all. We hate, despise, and fear death, and have great difficulty in facing it directly. This often appears as a lack of caring, a "coldness," and causes much resentment in the families of dying patients. Few know the pain the doctor experiences.

Thus there are different kinds of information to be revealed to the patient and the family, and different kinds of people on the receiving end. There is no definitive answer for the doctor except insofar as it is clarified by the patient or the family in a specific situation. If you fear you have a serious, perhaps fatal illness, ask your doctor and tell him point blank you want "the truth, the whole truth, and nothing but the truth, so help you God," if that, in fact, is what you want. If you fear the revelation, discuss that as well. Explain that if your doctor discovers you are dying, and you don't want to know, you are not to be told. But say *something*, because the doctor has no crystal ball, and among the courses in medical school there never was one called "Clairvoyance 101" (at least not in *my* medical school).

Unfortunately, there is a finite and specific time limit to such situations. If you keep postponing your little chat with your doctor because it is uncomfortable, there will— regrettably—be a day when it is simply too late, just as with the individual who never quite got around to telling his wife he really did love her, or the one who kept postponing the execution of a Last Will and Testament.

Throughout this book I will urge you to speak out about your dissatisfactions as a required first step toward rectifying them. I continue to advocate this method, not as infallible, but as the only sensible point of departure. If you rely on your doctor to try to fathom how much you want to know and what you can handle, if you permit or force him to mix his own feelings, anxieties, hangups, and personality in with *your* needs and desires, the chances that what he does and what you would like him to do will coincide are no greater than a throw of the dice. You have a *right* to know . . . what you want to know, no more, no less.

WHEN IS CONSENT "INFORMED"?

It is well to consider how much you would really *like* to know, along with how much the doctor feels like telling you, but this approach to the subject is a totally emotional and personal one. We have also to deal with a strictly medical–legal view of consent. At what point, granted that the wishes of the now-departed or the now-recovered patient were met, did the revelations become really *informed*? If the result of all this treatment mixed in among the talk was less than satisfactory, how much information is "enough" when examined by the microscope of hindsight? How much constitutes informed consent if the issue comes up in a courtroom?

The doctrine of informed consent in the 1980s is a grand example of the exercise of our constitutional right to free speech and free thought: nearly everyone involved has his or her own interpretation of what this means. It is, quite simply, a matter far from resolved in the legal sense. I suppose, after thinking about it carefully for years; writing about it for medical publications; expounding at great length to doctors, lawyers, patients, anyone who would listen to my endless rhetoric, that "enough" is in the mind of the beholder, somewhat akin to "beauty." Let us suppose that the doctor is comfortable that the significant dangers have been revealed to you and you have chosen to follow his or her recommendations nonetheless, confident in your own heart that your doctor wishes you only good results. Furthermore, if you as the patient are comfortable that you understand what is to be done, what might happen as a result, why alternative treatments are thought to be less desirable by *your* doctor for *your* situation, and what might happen if you refuse all treatment, *then* the consent has been informed without having become overkill.

WHY ARE WE TALKING ABOUT THIS AT ALL?

It is a source of amazement and scorn to consumer advocates that doctors should offer any resistance at all to providing full and complete disclosure of everything they know about a proposed treatment, operation, or medication. Those whose minds are inclined in such directions cannot fathom why, other than abuse of a doctor's Deity Complex, he or she would even think of withholding information from a patient. Those with more vivid imaginations or more highly developed paranoia dream up—and not infrequently write magazine or newspaper articles about—supposedly deliberate efforts of doctors to mask the dangers of procedures to avoid the sticky situation in which a patient refuses consent, thereby depriving the doctor of a fee. If you challenge such people on the absurdity of so crass an accusation when *generalized* to the whole profession (I'm sure there must be a few real occurrences like the Nevada case about the mastectomy), they quickly point to such a specific case and assume it applies to all doctors. Whatever your trade or profession, I'm sure I could with a little effort find some colleague of *yours*, someplace, who is an out-and-out crook, but that doesn't make you one. Professional generalizations are as meaningless as ethnic ones ("all Jews have hooked noses," "all Scandinavians are tall and blond," "all Italians are gangsters," "all Mexicans are fat and lazy"). You don't want your doctor to conduct "whole truth" discussions with you on the basis of all patients, and by the same application of equal justice, you should not view your doctor's motives as pertaining to all doctors, and certainly not as automatically equivalent to some flagrant abuse you heard or read about.

Some of the unacceptable reasons I have heard from doctors for withholding full disclosure (however they may be defining that elusive term) include:

1. Description of every possible side effect would result in every patient refusing consent.
2. Description of potential side effects will cause some patients to experience them automatically through psychosomatic suggestion.
3. Emotional patients will become too upset, so much so that they will not benefit from the treatment.
4. Hospital patients sign a "blanket consent" anyway, so why burden them with more details and stir up more trouble?
5. If one of the side effects revealed actually happens, the patient will be more likely to sue.
6. What patient can understand such technical and complex information anyway? The doctor knows best, and if the patient doesn't believe that, he or she should find another doctor.

Numbers 1, 2, and 3 are vague generalizations. Number 4 is quite meaningless, as we have already discussed. The value of such "blanket consent" forms lies more in helping to start your next barbecue fire. They are obsolete and should have been discarded long since. Number 5 is simply no excuse at all, merely an attempt at rationalization on the part of a few doctors, and number 6 is just hogwash, with no viable place in today's world. Not one of these "reasons" is justified, certainly not for general application, though one or another might be applicable in a specific situation or for a specific patient, and none is really in the best interests of the patient, with the same occasional exception. Even in the exceptional cases, what may be required is not a *withholding* of information but a *redirection* of it, toward some other member of the family better equipped to handle it.

There are bad effects of treatment that are *not* farfetched —anesthesia accidents and death during *any* kind of surgery, however "minor"; loss of hair, nausea, vomiting, and disability during initial stages of cancer chemotherapy— and they cannot be withheld from the patient. But the manner in which a physician communicates with and relates to his patients is also an important part of his professional skills, and the way he presents these real (but *not* necessarily universal or inevitable) effects of his proposed treatment as well as the way in which he puts them into proper perspective—loss of hair versus fairly certain death —must call upon these skills. The inability or unwillingness to present information in such a way that it enables the patient to both understand and accept such unhappy prospects does not in any way relieve the doctor of the responsibility to do so. Good communication is, in my mind, almost as important as the skill in wielding the scalpel or in selecting the dose of medication. One can hardly argue that a patient may suffer a cardiac arrest on the operating table or lose hair during chemotherapy only because the doctor "put the idea into his head."

There are many instances of illnesses caused by the doctor through harping on side effects, through inappropriate choice of medication, or a combination of medications that do not work well together. This is called *iatrogenic* disease, *disease born of the physician*. Withholding important information or seeking to obtain consent that is not based on full disclosure of relevant information to the patient, however, is not a satisfactory or acceptable way of avoiding such unfortunate occurrences.

There are certainly some highly emotional patients who, in the judgment of a sincere doctor, might take adverse information about risks rather poorly and whose general condition might actually become worse through exaggerated worry. Here it is reasonable to expect that the doctor will use some discretion in modifying "full disclosure" since his primary interest should, after all, be the well-being and best interests of the patient. Any doctor concerned about legal liability should take pains to provide the information to close relatives and then carefully consider *their* wishes and opinions about telling the patient. It's like the old trick of big corporations or government bodies when a touchy decision must be made. A *committee* is formed so that the responsibility, if things go wrong, is spread around among many persons instead of resting on the head of one. Ultimately, though, there is always a place where, as President Harry Truman liked to say, "the buck stops," where the ultimate responsibility must lie. You should remember that while you may demand the privilege and the right to make decisions about your medical care, the doctor bears the ultimate responsibility for them. When things go awry, "the buck" comes to rest in the doctor's lap.

The doctor may, therefore, if he feels strongly that your decision is really wrong, elect to dump you as a patient, by following the proper legal procedure, explaining that he cannot in good conscience be a party to your care when, in his opinion, your decision will be harmful to you, and by giving you formal notice and sufficient time to find another doctor who may be more understanding—or may simply care less. When you seek the other doctor, the one who will "agree" with you, do not lose sight of the fact that this doctor may be doing you a great disservice and may not, by any means, be a "better doctor" because he or she agrees with you.

WHEN CAN OR MUST CONSENT BE GRANTED BY OTHERS?

There are a precious few instances in which consent may be given by someone other than the patient, and a few in which it *must* be granted by someone else. The most obvious one that comes immediately to mind is when the patient is unconscious, and the next is when minors are concerned. This latter situation has undergone some remarkable changes in attitude in recent years, however, and I will address these new concepts regarding the rights of minors in Chapter 10. The facts may startle you, and the new outlooks are so far reaching that they demand a chapter of their own.

In general, however, persons under the legal age of majority for their state are called infants in legal terminology, and the law assumes that such individuals have neither the right nor the capacity to decide their own fate. Consequently, a doctor must obtain the consent of a parent or, if this is not relevant, of the legal guardian of the child. There are exceptions, and they fall into the category of simple common sense. Where treatment is urgent or necessary to save the child's life and a parent is not immediately available, every state recognizes the right and the *duty* of the physician to administer to the child first and worry about "consent" afterward. In other words, the doctor has the right to assume temporarily the role of a parent, doing what the physician believes an informed parent would want and readily consent to if available. It does *not* mean that the child may give consent on his or her own except in those special circumstances to which I alluded above and which will be dealt with in Chapter 10.

Cases are frequently reported in the newspapers in which parents have refused permission for certain treatment to children, most commonly blood transfusions, where the religious beliefs of the parents prohibit such treatment.

Doctors who believe the life of the child is at stake may petition the court with the argument that if the child had the capacity to understand the risk to his or her life, the *child* might not agree with the religious views of the parents. Sometimes the courts agree, make the child temporarily a ward of the court, and, acting in place of the parent, grant the consent. Sometimes they do not.

An equally difficult situation is that in which the patient's mental competence to understand the ramifications and risks of the treatment versus no treatment is questioned. The patient may be mentally ill, mentally deficient, old, sick, and/or possibly senile, and either doctor or relatives seek to be appointed legal guardians. Such situations are extremely difficult to resolve even by the courts. Sometimes the results leave the appointed guardians with a great sense of guilt for having intervened at all, especially if hindsight reveals that the decision that seemed so "right" at the time didn't benefit the patient. One must be guided by one's conscience in such matters, for if the decision is ultimately shown to have been "wrong" (inappropriate), the conscience will demand too high a price.

The by now classic case that revolved around the issues of consent by others as well as "the right to die" was the widely publicized matter of Karen Ann Quinlan (In Re Quinlan, 70 N.J. 10, 1976), adjudged just one block from where I sit writing this book. Karen, a twenty-one-year-old, was comatose from brain damage of undetermined origin, and was apparently being kept alive by a respirator device. In keeping with their religious principles the parents petitioned to be named legal guardians of the unconscious girl so that they might arrange to stop the use of the respirator to keep her alive. The physicians had refused to stop using the respirator, believing that Karen would die as a result and such removal would not conform to standards of medical practice. The court ruled for the parents, holding that in its opinion there was no hope that the patient would return to "a cognitive state" (conscious and aware of the world around her), and no criminal or civil liability would be attached to the act of any participant in the decision, whether guardian, physician, hospital, or others. Incidentally, the respirator *was* disconnected and Karen lives on in a total vegetative state, much to the surprise of all concerned.

Another interesting aspect of "consent by others" was argued in another case in the same court before the same judge some two years later. In this matter (In Re Quackenbush, 156 Sup 282, N.J. 1978), a seventy-two-year-old man, divorced with no children and no living parents or siblings, was brought to the hospital with gangrene of both legs. Amputation was indicated and there was little disagreement that in its absence Mr. Quackenbush would die within weeks. He refused and the hospital, believing it was acting in the best interest of the patient, petitioned for the appointment of a guardian to grant consent for the operation. After due consideration—including a personal visit by the judge to the hospital patient—the court concluded that Mr. Quackenbush was competent to understand the nature of his decision. The judge ruled that the extent of invasion of the patient's body was so great as to supersede the state's interest in preservation of life. Rather, the patient's right to privacy and to decide his own future regardless of the consequences should prevail. Judge Muir therefore ruled: "Quackenbush . . . as a mentally competent individual, has the right to make his informed choice concerning the operation and I will not interfere with that choice."

In bygone days it was the custom to insist on a husband's consent in addition to the wife/patient's consent for certain types of treatment, especially where surgery was indicated or contemplated that might render the wife infertile. This "right" of a husband to have the final say over his spouse's childbearing capacity is rather obsolete legally, though to avoid potential problems where *either* spouse seeks sterilization, doctors will usually request the concurrence of the other spouse. If you feel strongly about your private right to make decisions about your own fertility without consulting your spouse, and your doctor will not agree to a sterilization procedure without your spouse's written consent, find another doctor who will. Neither point of view has the firm backing of law. A similar situation prevails on the subject of abortion, but fewer physicians bother about the husband's consent, probably because it is not a procedure that permanently alters the reproductive state. All such matters should rightfully belong to the individual's conscience, not to the personal prejudices of the physician. A startling new set of legal and moral thoughts has emerged in recent years regarding patients still adolescents and under the legal *age* of consent, to be discussed at length in Chapter 10.

In determining whether a patient should be relieved of the right and privilege of determining his own fate, the courts will *start* by assuming that any adult individual who, faced with a choice of treatment or probable death, chooses death, is not in full command of his or her senses, or such a decision would not be made. This is only the starting point, however, and there are extenuating circumstances that lead the courts to the opposite conclusion. It is now known as "The Right To Die."

WHEN SHOULD YOU GRANT CONSENT?

If we accept the premise that you have every right to know what is to be done to you and to decide whether you want it done or not, what guidelines do you need to make such decisions in an intelligent manner?

You will want to know, of course, just what in general it is your doctor proposes to do to you. You want to know, for example, that your doctor says you should have your gall bladder removed, not that he proposes to make a four-inch incision in the right upper quadrant of the abdominal wall, position two retractors, free the gall bladder from under the liver, and so on. You should know what risks are involved if you agree to the treatment, but equally important, what risks are involved if you do not! You may ask about alternative treatments, those you may have read or heard about as well as those known only to your doctor, and why he feels the proposed treatment is best for you. Forget what Mrs. Smith's doctor did to *her*. The symptoms may have sounded the same and the diagnosis may even have been the same, but some or all of the other conditions, factors, and contingencies may have been entirely different.

It is most likely that your doctor has chosen a treatment not at random, or because it generates a large fee for him, or even because he gets his "kicks" that way, but because he has carefully thought out your individual case and feels the treatment is best for you, all things considered. Among the "all things . . ." are your medical history, your ability to cope with certain adversities, other coexistent diseases you may have or medications you are taking that are necessary for other conditions, your age, your general health, your family and social situation, and whether another procedure with greater risk is worth trying. It may make sense to do an extensive repair of a hernia in a thirty-five-year man who must earn a living as a laborer, but it may make more sense to manage conservatively a similar hernia in an eighty-five-year old confined to a nursing home for whom the quality of life will remain unchanged after the surgery. There is no good reason why your doctor should not be willing to explain to you how he happened to select the treatment he proposes. A contented, believing, and trusting patient is always more pleasant to deal with, and often recovers from his illness or surgery better or faster than a skeptical patient does.

Finally, if the answers you receive leave you with nagging

doubts, the second opinion route may provide the answer so long as you do not carry it out indefinitely. Even in quite difficult cases (there is always a rare exception) there is little to be gained beyond the *third* opinion. By then you should have a clear idea what learned and experienced professionals consider best for you.

In earlier chapters I have discussed the criteria by which you should grant consent. Yet some treatment alternatives remain the subject of heated controversy within the medical profession, at least at this time, and at times also between physicians and consumer advocates or those deeply committed to women's rights movements. The one you may hear about most frequently deals with the tragedy of breast cancer.

For decades radical mastectomy, the complete removal of a breast along with nearby lymphatic (glandular) tissue and even some muscle, was the treatment of choice for breast cancer, followed by either radiation therapy or chemotherapy, or both. More recently, some have advocated a less extreme method, a simple mastectomy, which is the removal of the breast but much less of the surrounding structures (which claims no worse record for five-year survival of the patients), or even simply the removal of the tumor itself with subsequent radiation and/or chemotherapy to kill any small growths in nearby or distant areas. Even the big-words-only doctors have come to call this procedure a lumpectomy.

The unfortunate part of this controversy is the irrevocable nature of the decision. If a less debilitating procedure than radical mastectomy is performed and we learn, with the usual hindsight, that it was not enough, we can't turn the clock back and do it over. Most doctors would choose radical or simple mastectomy or modified radical mastectomy (somewhere between the two) for their own wives or mothers. That should probably tell us something, at least as much as the intellectual and scientific arguments propounded by those in favor and those opposed to the classic radical procedure.

Doctors *do* know how psychologically distressing it is to a woman to lose a breast. It is not an operation undertaken lightly by any surgeon I have ever met, though his concern may be adequately expressed only to colleagues, not to patients. I have seen surgeons weeping openly in the operating room when the biopsy reveals a well-established malignancy with potential or actual spread of the cancer into the nearby tissues and the mastectomy becomes mandatory for survival.

But we are talking about *consent* here, and if you feel strongly that a lumpectomy would be sufficient and your doctor feels just as strongly that he cannot in good conscience treat you in this manner, you both must simply own up to your individual feelings and part company without anger. But do talk to other *professional* people before you make your decision. At the bottom line, would you choose to die unmutilated with your body intact, or to live with one bra cup filled by a silicone or foam pad?

If your doctor explains everything fully to you but you are uncertain about the meaning of certain things, this is no time to be shy. Ask, and ask again, until you are sure you know and understand everything. As long as you are embarked on the road of comprehension and informed consent, do your best to understand. Then make your informed decision, based on the facts, your instincts, and your doctor's skilled professional advice.

CHAPTER 5

HOW TO PROCEED

CHOICE OF ATTORNEY

You have read through the preceding chapters and are convinced that you have good and substantial reason to believe that your doctor has been negligent in your care. You feel that the injury done to you was not mere chance, not the imprecision of current medical treatment, not a result of your having expected too much, and not a result of your own acts against your doctor's advice ("contributory negligence"). You want to sue, and are convinced that you are entitled to monetary compensation. What now?

The most important factor in this situation will be your choice of lawyer. You believe that your family doctor is the best choice for routine medical supervision but that an experienced cardiovascular surgeon is preferred for open-heart surgery; an experienced gynecologist for a hysterectomy; a highly competent and experienced psychiatrist for treatment of schizophrenia; and a very skilled and experienced neurosurgeon for removal of a brain tumor.

With the same reasoning, your family lawyer is an excellent choice for preparation of wills, title closings for your new house, and even for suing the neighbor whose basement sump pump discharges into your vegetable garden. An attorney skilled and experienced in medical malpractice cases is equally as important to your chances of success with this lawsuit as the neurosurgeon's skills are to the successful removal of the brain tumor. It is unclear why patients demand the very highest level of skill and expertise from their doctor, but when he or she falls short of their expectations, retain an attorney with little or no experience in professional liability cases (the legal name for malpractice) to pursue their case for them. Just as there are many areas of medicine in which the special talents of the family doctor are preferred to the impersonal and restricted expertise of the specialist, and conversely, others where only the highly specialized and narrowly focused knowledge of the specialist is an absolute necessity, so the same principles apply in the practice of law. It is not at all unusual to discover much later that your proposed malpractice suit was won or lost at the moment of decision when you selected your lawyer.

But how can you make such a decision intelligently? In many locales, doctors are permitted to list their specialty in the telephone directory yellow pages. Lawyers still rarely advertise, though recent government rulings and court decisions permitting advertising by attorneys are gradually changing this. You might ask around among your friends as you would when seeking a new doctor, but many people contemplating a lawsuit against their doctor prefer not to talk about it much in social circles. One never knows who might be a friend or a loyal patient of that doctor. In addition, while personality is an important consideration in your relationship with your doctor, it plays a much smaller role in your relationship with your attorney. As in the medical profession, the true judgment of a lawyer's competence can usually be made only by other lawyers or, if you could get them to talk about it (hardly likely, considering), by judges before whom they have appeared to try a case.

Your own family lawyer is often in a good position to recommend an attorney who has gained respect for the skillful management of malpractice cases. But few lawyers actually limit their practice to malpractice cases, and in general the practice of specialized lawyers is not as restricted as that of medical specialists, who are expected to spend 90 percent of their time or more practicing their specialty to the exclusion of other fields of medicine. Consequently, the family lawyer may be reluctant to refer you to another attorney who might later also assume the duties of family lawyer to you.

The local bar association emerges as your best source for finding an attorney who is, at least, experienced in this exacting field. Every county has a bar association that will readily provide you with the names of several attorneys in the area known to be knowledgeable in this type of law. A brief interview with one or more of them should show you clearly which one you would like to handle your case, even if your decision *is* now reduced to the level of compatible personalities. At least you will be choosing among recognized experts in the field.

PREPARING THE CASE

Your attorney's first task will be to become informed of the nature of your complaint, the reasons for your dissatisfaction, and your allegations or accusations about your doctor's performance or conduct. Your attorney will be taking the history in much the same manner as your doctor does. Armed with this information, with *your* version of what happened, and assuming for the moment that what you have told him is truthful and accurate, your attorney must now take certain informative steps to determine if there is any reasonable basis for a lawsuit. Since an attorney is not a medical expert, he must seek assistance from medically knowledgeable persons who can advise him if the treatment you complained of is up to the usual standards, if it might or might not be, depending on the circumstances, or if it is clearly not consistent with today's level of medical practice. Consequently, if your first choice of attorney listens to you briefly, takes some but not many notes, and assures you that you have an excellent case that will result in a substantial financial award for you from the doctor, it might be a good idea to pay him the initial consultation fee and try the second attorney on your list. With the single possible exception of those cases where "the fact speaks for itself" (like the case of an instrument left inside the patient's body), no one can be *that* sure about a medical matter or the outcome of a medical malpractice suit, especially if he is not a physician.

An attorney who frequently handles malpractice cases knows of medical experts in various specialties, and at times, medical–legal consultants. These latter individuals, though few in number, can position the quality of medical care quite precisely in the legal world because they have been educated in both fields. Such assistance gives the lawyer clear insight into the merits of the case.

Your attorney may also wish to obtain copies of hospital records, prescriptions, or other relevant written matter to clarify or confirm details of the story you have related. Only after having been fully informed about the matter from you, from the written records, and from the advice of medical consultants can your attorney offer you an educated guess as to the merits of your case and the chances of success in court.

Your attorney may also wish to research the legal literature to determine the outcome of other similar cases in
your locality as well as in other states. Our system of legal
justice is heavily dependent on prior cases ("precedent")
that more or less resemble the facts of this new case.

KEEPING AN OPEN MIND

If you have selected your attorney wisely, and he advises
you not to pursue the matter, it would be prudent to heed
this advice. A lawyer's principal income is derived from
bringing lawsuits to trial and winning them, or settling
them out of court. When an attorney suggests that both of
you would be wasting time by going to court, this is advice
that deserves your careful consideration, much as does the
advice from a surgeon who recommends against an operation. Do not scorn either this lawyer or this surgeon; you
have met a professional of integrity who is to be praised
and honored for professional truthfulness.

An open mind is an essential factor. Though you may
feel wronged, though you may feel angry and resentful,
bear in mind that not every such emotion, however justified it may be, has an act of *negligence* as its cause. As I
have stressed repeatedly, no doctor is truly a god (though
a few persist in thinking so), and no doctor, however competent and expert, has the absolute ability to cure every
patient. Consequently, not every case of utter disappointment with your doctor's performance or results is a case
of negligence, incompetence, or malpractice. The loss of a
loved one, for example, is a deeply wounding, hurtful experience. Similarly, the diagnosis of a terminal or incurable
illness in oneself, one's child, or parent is excruciatingly
painful. It is customary and perfectly normal for people
to react with a predictable sequence of emotions. First
comes the shock and the refusal to believe. After this comes

the anger ("Why, God, why *me*?"), and it is this anger, coupled with a little guilt that a different life-style might perhaps have avoided the tragedy, that can only too easily be focused on someone close to you at the time. Some people use a spouse as the object of anger, guilt, and frustration. Some use the doctor.

My advice as an impartial observer is not to visit a lawyer for a while after the possible malpractice incident has occurred. Labor relations experts recognize the need for a "cooling-off period" when things have become too hot, and the philosophy applies equally well to lawsuits, especially malpractice ones. Of course, you should not wait too long, for time diminishes not only accurate memory, but the availability of witnesses and the possibility of recreating the incident as accurately as possible. Perhaps one to three months is a good rule of thumb. You will be able to be more objective at that time, and to hear your attorney's advice with a receptive mind. Some states require that the plaintiff serve a "Notice of Intent to Sue" on the intended defendant, but prohibit a suit from actually being filed until a specified period of time has elapsed after the notice was served. California, for example, requires the passage of ninety days. This is tantamount to a mandatory cooling-off period, and frankly doesn't sound like a bad idea, in theory at least. No figures are available, however, to reflect how many proposed lawsuits are dropped during the cooling-off period.

Of course, if you have serious reservations about the wisdom of your attorney's advice, seek a second opinion. If both attorneys agree, acknowledge their expertise and the wisdom of their recommendations. Patients who persist despite recurring legal advice have probably not really been wronged at all but have other motives for the lawsuit. If they search long enough, such people can always find a lawyer who will file the suit for them.

MEDICAL SOCIETY AND PRETRIAL REVIEWS

Most county medical societies, many county bar associations, and some judicial jurisdictions provide for informal review of potential or newly filed malpractice actions before they are actually put on the court calendar and irrevocably scheduled for trial. Such reviews are extremely helpful both in clarifying the merits of a suit and thereby possibly leading to an early out-of-court settlement, and in identifying cases that have no merit and are thus doomed to failure. These reviews help to eliminate the emotional, financial, costly, and prolonged drains on patient, doctor, and two sets of lawyers.

In the course of such reviews, each side has an opportunity to present its side of the situation, and sometimes to present expert testimony to support its contentions. It is a foolish mistake to think that the members of a medical society or bar association (or combined) review committees are there only to protect their own interests or those of their professional colleagues. History reveals that the eventual outcome of most malpractice cases heard by such committees and later brought to trial is just what the committee predicted, whether or not the plaintiff followed the advice of the committee. If the review panel feels the case has no merit but the patient pursues it anyway, the case usually ends with a verdict in favor of the defendant. If the panel feels the case is fully justified but the doctor does not agree to an out-of-court settlement, he most commonly loses in court.

Pretrial reviews or hearings, held before a judge or panel without many of the formalities and rules of a full courtroom trial, are a good preview of the actual performance. As a result of the pretrial hearing, a few details of the case might be modified, some additional evidence or testimony might be developed for presentation in court, but by and large the results will be similar, months or years and thousands of dollars in costs later, to the informal decision rendered at the hearing. In fact, an attorney who is enthusiastic about bringing a case to trial might have his enthusiasm dampened somewhat after a pretrial hearing that results in a recommendation strongly in favor of the other party. The attorney's efforts will usually turn suddenly toward attempts to effect a smaller out-of-court settlement, but this is not always easy to do. After all, the "other side" is also present at the hearing, and it, too, has heard the recommendations. Now is a good time to stop and reflect on the wisdom of your actions. In a sense, you have seen "the handwriting on the wall"; believe it.

In certain states, the pretrial hearing has been made mandatory specifically for the expeditious handling of medical malpractice cases. In the State of New Jersey, for example, Section 4:21 of the Civil Practice Rules was adopted in 1978 to require a mandatory pretrial conference as part of the legal procedure for professional liability claims against members of the medical profession. (See Appendix 3.) The rules state that the procedure was adopted "with the view toward discouraging baseless actions and encouraging settlement of those actions based on reasonable medical probability. . . ." Hearings are held before a panel consisting of a judge, a doctor, and a lawyer. The panel's verdict may be admissible as evidence in any eventual trial of the case if the panel decision is unanimous, but the decision is not binding on the trial judge or jury, who are instructed to give it such importance as it seems to deserve when placed into perspective with the rest of the evidence presented during the actual trial. Thus we have a situation in which the *courts*, not the doctors, have admitted that they are burdened with malpractice cases, many of which are without justification or merit, and have taken steps in conjunction with bar associations and medical societies (who provide the doctor and lawyer members of the review panel) to weed out the worthy cases from the others, and to seek an early settlement without trial if at all possible.

BRINGING THE CASE INTO THE COURTROOM

A student's performance on a final exam is more dependent on preparation than on general brilliance. Likewise, the outcome of a legal dispute is heavily contingent on the adequacy of the preparations by each of the lawyers before they enter the courtroom.

Such preparations take many forms. The accumulation of copies of relevant written records such as hospital charts, prescriptions, pharmacist's transcripts, or notes of telephone conversations with the doctor, are of great importance, for they permit the attorney to determine how much written documentation will be available to confirm and support or to weaken and deny the client's allegations. As I noted earlier, there is nothing like a written record to remove all doubt or difference of opinion on a specific point or detail. If you consent to have them released, your lawyer can usually obtain such records without undue difficulty, although it may be necessary to call into play certain legal procedures to require that the parties holding the records produce them for use in the case.

Legal research into similar cases and their verdicts may be helpful, and an attorney experienced in handling this type of lawsuit should be sufficiently knowledgeable about medical matters to engage in some relatively superficial research into the medical literature for obvious confirmations or denials of your allegations. For example, if you claim that your doctor prescribed a dose of medication that was too high, reference to medical texts might reveal that the dose, while not the most common, is well within the normal range of doses for that medication in certain circumstances, or well within the government-approved recommended dose range of the manufacturer. Or, conversely, it might clearly indicate that such a dose could only have been prescribed through error, carelessness, or a total lack of knowledge about the drug on the part of the doctor.

If the case still seems plausible at this point, your attorney will wish to seek out the expert advice of medical specialists in the field of your illness for their opinion on the adequacy of the care rendered by your doctor. Was it up to expected standards? Would other physicians in the community of similar training have managed the case in the same way, in another alternate and optional but not necessarily *superior* way, or in a totally different manner?

Expert witnesses will be sought who are willing to testify in your behalf during the trial. These may or may not be the same persons who acted as medical consultants to the attorney, or who testified at the pretrial hearing if one was held, but they should be recognized experts in their specialty—the more widely known the better. In cases where there is the possibility of large sums of money being awarded, nationally or internationally famous specialists may be flown in from thousands of miles away to testify. Needless to say, this costs a good deal of money, for such experts are entitled to fees consistent with their reputation, plus reimbursement of expenses incurred for the trip. By the same reasoning, if you elect to retain a famous attorney from a distant state to assist in trying the case, that will certainly involve a high fee for services rendered.

TV shows and movies usually portray courtroom dramatics as the deciding factor in verdicts. They rarely influence the court that much in real life. Such theatrical lawyers bear little resemblance to the real world. Far more critical to the outcome of the case are the following, listed in what is in my opinion their order of importance:

1. Reality and justification of the allegations
2. Confirmation of the plaintiff's allegations by written records, especially those of third parties
3. Substantiation of the plaintiff's allegations by expert medical witnesses
4. Effective presentation of the case to the court by your attorney

The absence, or successful discrediting by the opposing lawyer, of any one of these, strikes at the very foundations of the case and weakens it immeasurably. The absence or discrediting of two or more of them usually dooms the case.

The judge, occupying an honorable position on the bench by reason of recognition by peers of his or her experience, wisdom, and expertise in points and matters of law, is not an expert in medical matters, and would be the first to admit it. The judge, therefore, relies heavily on the testimony of the expert witnesses put on the stand by each party to the controversy. The jury probably does so even more. Here, as in so many other facets of life, *quality*, not quantity, is the essence of success. Clear, concise, and truthful testimony, given without hesitancy, by a doctor recognized and respected by *his* peers as holding a high degree of expertise in his field is far more useful to your cause than a parade of self-styled "experts" who contradict themselves and each other, answer questions only after considerable hesitation and prodding by the attorney, or become defensive and angry when their testimony is questioned or their contradictions are pointed out. Such emotional reactions on the witness stand are so common (and so damaging) that in some types of trials the defendant's attorney is not required to call his client to the witness stand, out of fear that the client's emotional involvement will affect his testimony and hinder his own case.

Civil cases of any nature usually consume prolonged periods of time before they come to trial. The courts of most areas of the country are overloaded with civil suits of all kinds in our litigation-minded society. A suit filed in Boulder, Colorado, in 1979 by a son against his mother alleging "parental malpractice" was countered with another suit by the mother against the son's psychiatrist for medical malpractice claiming that he had encouraged the son to sue his mother "for therapeutic reasons." Both cases will eventually have to be heard. Because of these long delays, the more information that can be committed to writing or obtained in writing in one form or another, and the less the case hinges on someone's memory, the stronger it will be in the eyes of the court, and the better its chances of a successful outcome. You will recall that I advocated a brief cooling-off period before the initial visit to your lawyer. But this advice was accompanied by a warning not to prolong the period unnecessarily. The sooner someone goes to work on your case, the more thorough will be the preparation, and if your cause is justified, the better your chances of a verdict in your favor.

Another very cogent reason for not unduly delaying your initial contact with a lawyer is the fact that the law prescribes a finite and limited period of time in which you may file a suit. This time is specified in the statute of limitations of your state, and varies in length from state to state (see pages 200 and 201 for a state-by-state listing). In some states it may be as short as one year, in others, several years. But there are a few strings attached that determine the point at which you begin the counting.

The courts in different states do not agree on the interpretation of when the statute of limitations begins to run, when "the clock is started." Some courts hold that you count from the time the alleged wrongful act was committed. Others maintain that it begins only when the physician completes or terminates treatment of the patient, when the physician–patient relationship ceases to exist, while still others hold to the interpretation that the time period for filing a suit does not begin until *the injury is discovered*. If you only learn five years after an operation that an instrument was left inside your body, and your state's statute of limitations for malpractice cases is one year, you have one year from the time the wrongful act was discovered in which to file a lawsuit. Your lawyer is the only person properly able to advise you on the details of this matter. If your suit is not filed in a timely manner, within the rigid and inflexible interpretation of the laws of your state, it can be dismissed as a faulty case upon request of the defendant.

In cases where the injury is done to a child, some states hold that the statute of limitations does not come into play until the child reaches the legal age of majority. Thus, in certain circumstances a malpractice case can theoretically be filed against a doctor twenty or twenty-five years after the wrongful act was committed.

Suits for breach of contract usually have different, and most commonly *longer*, periods for filing under the statute of limitations, and other types of lawsuits will also have different periods of time specified. It is important to know just what kind of a suit you may file. It is equally important to ensure that the proper physician or physicians have been named as defendants. If your first choices are incorrect, by the time the case comes to trial and you learn of the error, it may be too late to refile for a different lawsuit. This is no place for any do-it-yourself legal practice.

COMPENSATION, OR A GET-RICH-QUICK SCHEME?

The size of the award, the actual number of dollars requested in your lawsuit, should be determined through serious discussion with your attorney. While the amount of money occasionally awarded in malpractice suits literally boggles the mind, you must remember that such cases are few and rare, and are publicized by the news media *because* they are exceptional. Most malpractice suits won by the plaintiff represent more reasonable compensation for an injury negligently caused by the doctor, and usually do not exceed four or five figures. It is the enormous *number* of malpractice cases and the staggering *total* of awards rather than the few extraordinarily large awards that has caused the malpractice crisis.

In determining an award once a verdict has been rendered in favor of the plaintiff, the court will take into consideration the true and realistic loss suffered by the plaintiff. For example, such considerations might be loss of earning power temporarily or permanently (and at what stage of one's life it occurred); loss of the companionship of a husband or wife disabled by the wrongful act or worse; expenses incurred in rectifying the mistake or the negligent care, or in care of a disabled person, etc. If the court concludes that the doctor was not only guilty of failure to perform duties at the level expected of him, but was also willfully negligent or made conscious efforts to cover up any negligence, it may order the doctor to pay punitive damages as well, and this will inflate the award considerably. The punitive damages are quite often larger than the actual damages.

Feelings of sympathy or pity for the plaintiff elicited in the courtroom by the exhibition of, for example, a crippled child or a deformed young woman, particularly in those states where the *jury* has the power to set or recommend the amount of the award, can occasionally lead to awards far beyond what appears reasonable, but this is not an everyday occurrence. For the most part, a judge is not interested in helping you take revenge by financially ruining the doctor. Not only the decision to file suit but also the amount requested should relate honestly to the realities of the extent of injury, the degree to which the doctor caused it, and the willfulness or knowledge of the doctor in acting negligently or incompetently, and should not be based solely on a desire for revenge. Such honest appraisals of the case will do much to prevent later disappointment when the award is made and is but a small fraction of the amount you had requested or your lawyer had led you to expect. Most judges pay only minimal attention to the amount mentioned in filing the suit, and in some states the plaintiff is not even permitted to specify an amount. Such cases can only ask for "such compensation and damages as the court may see fit to award." In others, a specific amount of money may be stated in the suit, but the amount may not be revealed to the jury during the trial.

Some states have attempted to address the crisis and to limit the steadily increasing size of awards in malpractice cases by enacting statutory limits on the amount of money that can be awarded. These statutes are known as "cap" laws because they place a "cap" on the monetary awards. Many of these laws, however, are being challenged as unconstitutional because they deny the injured party free access to the judicial system for adequate compensation in proportion to the loss or injury, and it is highly doubtful that cap laws will remain in effect.

Bear in mind as well that any lawsuit, however justified or clear-cut it might have appeared, *can* be lost in the courtroom. If the matter had been so black and white, it probably would never have reached the trial stage. Rules of legal practice permit an attorney to advance certain costs of preparing a case, settling up with the client periodically, or when the case is concluded. The attorney is not, however, permitted to have a personal vested interest by risking his own money. Therefore, if you go to court and lose, your attorney still has a right to be *reimbursed* for the expenses laid out (in addition to any *fee*), and this has nothing to do with whether or not you won the case.

Proper preparation of a simple malpractice case costs at least $2,500, and now averages more than $5,000. Many lawyers will request an advance against these expenses, but whether your lawyer does or not, he is entitled to be reimbursed for expenses at some point. Rest assured that your lawyer will enforce the right to be reimbursed with all the skills and talents of the legal profession, and with considerably more vigor than any doctor might have exerted to collect a fee. If your case is weak and your finances even weaker, if you cannot comfortably afford to pay your legal expenses unless you win the case, and winning is somewhat dubious, think twice, and still another time, before proceeding. Have confidence in the advice received about your chances of success. If you don't have that much confidence in your advisor, better get another one, or at least another opinion, before you risk a significant sum of money.

There is one last common misunderstanding on the part of plaintiffs that needs clarification before I leave the subject of financial awards. When the court grants a specified sum of money "plus costs," the costs referred to are the payments specified by the state for filing the case, serving the summons, and other such expenses. They do *not* include *your attorney's fee* or the expenses the attorney incurred in your behalf in bringing expert witnesses into court to testify in support of your cause. Any fees beyond the court costs mentioned above will be deducted from your award. Some states have a predetermined formula set by the courts or recommended by the state bar association for calculating the size of the fee that is based on a fixed percentage (most commonly in the neighborhood of 30 percent) or on a sliding scale of percentages of the amount won. In other areas, this must be settled between client and attorney, and intelligence suggests that it be clearly agreed upon in advance.

The percentage method is better known by its common name, the "contingency fee" (i.e., the lawyer's fee is *contingent* on the amount he or she succeeds in winning for you). This is blamed by many people, particularly doctors, for causing frivolous lawsuits encouraged by attorneys who have small practices, nothing better to do, and a lot to gain but little to lose by pursuing every case that comes to their attention. On the other hand, a study conducted in the early 1970s and published in 1976 by the U.S. Department of Health, Education and Welfare (HEW) (see page 28)—and reviewed and commented on in another 1976 HEW report by a renowned Harvard professor of legal medicine, William J. Curran[1]—concluded after interviewing many attorneys across the nation that the contingency fee may more often than not result in some very worthy cases failing to obtain legal representation because the potential award is low, and the lawyer cannot therefore expect to earn a satisfactory fee. Thus a truly wronged or injured poor person might not be able to find an experienced attorney willing to file suit if the potential award were too small. The survey showed that few plaintiffs' attorneys thought that the contingency fee system increased their acceptance of frivolous suits. However, these same attorneys, responding to another question in the same survey, felt that as many as two-thirds of the cases they *did* accept were without significant evidence of real malpractice. No plaintiff's attorney surveyed thought he or she earned "too much" under the contingency system, but 20 percent of the defense attorneys thought that attorneys on the plaintiffs' side earned an excessive amount.

There are those who claim that some surgeons recommend unnecessary operations if the patient thinks the operation might be needed and if the patient has Blue Cross, Blue Shield, and major medical insurance coverage. Apart from a few bad apples in both professions, I have difficulty believing that a self-respecting professional, either doctor or lawyer, would descend to this level. A competent attor-

[1] Curran, William J. "How Lawyers Handle Medical Malpractice Cases: An Analysis of an Important Medicolegal Study." Washington, D.C.: U.S. Government Printing Office, 1976.

ney spends a great deal of time and money preparing a case, and would be quite unwilling to do this unless he thought his case was justified, or at least that the chances of winning were excellent.

A novel situation has cropped up a few times in the past year or two that bears watching. If it establishes a trend, it could act to further prevent the frivolous malpractice suit or the continuation of a case by an attorney when disinterested third parties all agree that it has little or no merit. This new occurrence is called the countersuit. In it, the doctor, once exonerated of any wrongdoing, and convinced that there was no basis for suing in the first place, countersues the patient and/or the patient's attorney for abuse of the legal process. Among the first few such cases won by the doctor, at least one was subsequently overturned by a court of appeals. It is really too early to tell whether such actions will be upheld in general, and if so, whether they will in fact have any significant bearing on the malpractice situation.

WHAT TO DO ABOUT OUTSTANDING BILLS

If you have finally reached the point where a lawsuit seems the only alternative, what should you do about your outstanding bill? The answer to this question depends on what the bill is for.

If the only outstanding unpaid charges on your account are for treatment that is disputed, for treatment that you feel was incompetent or negligent, the charge that will be the subject of your malpractice suit, you may safely postpone payment until the dispute is resolved. Your lawyer should advise the doctor that the bill will be paid only if the case is settled in the doctor's favor. But beware of using this as a means of not paying bills at all. If you lose the case and still refuse to pay, you may be subjected to legal action, may suffer the reporting of unfavorable credit information, and may even be accused of contempt of court if payment of the bill was mentioned in the court's decision. You could, of course, pay the bill and settle up after the lawsuit. Be aware, however, that up to the point you raised objection to the manner of treatment, the charges were totally justified and the doctor has every right to collect them. Your doctor did not guarantee success, only competent care.

When the outstanding amounts on your account are for prior visits or treatments that are not part of the disputed situation, you are obligated to pay them. You cannot use the excuse that the doctor was incompetent at a later date for refusing to pay prior charges. The care for which those charges were levied *was* satisfactory, and the doctor expended time, money, and knowledge to render the care.

Obviously, if the outstanding bills include amounts for care of other members of your family that, for convenience of all concerned, are combined into a single "family" bill, you have no excuse whatsoever to refuse to pay them. In fact, refusal to pay such charges entirely unrelated to the dispute lends some credence to the suspicion that your underlying motive for filing the suit may be little more than to wipe out your entire unpaid bill. It does happen, and you can hardly blame the doctor for making a serious effort later to damage your credit standing along with any other vigorous efforts to collect the money due.

What if your refusal to pay the bill for the disputed treatment or care that is the subject of your lawsuit has already resulted in the doctor turning over the account to a credit bureau, collection agency, or attorney for collection? Your best action is to advise *your* attorney, who will, in turn, inform the collection agency of the impending lawsuit. It is likely that the agency will suggest to the doctor that this is not the appropriate time to pursue rigorous collection efforts (and if the agency doesn't, your doctor's lawyer certainly will!), but that collection efforts are best suspended until the dispute has been resolved one way or another. Just remember that it is a temporary reprieve, and you may have to pay up heavily if you lose the suit or if you later decide to drop it.

If you had it to do over again, would you still prefer suing the doctor to some other, less nerve-wracking alternative? The next chapter will examine some ways in which you might avoid becoming involved in a lawsuit in some future relationship with a doctor.

CHAPTER 6

HOW TO AVOID LAWSUITS NEXT TIME

WHAT WENT WRONG?

Let us assume for a moment that a lawsuit is giving you no pleasure, that it is causing you some anxiety and hardship, and that you wish there could have been "a better way." No doubt it is too late to do much about your present problem, but how could the lawsuit have been avoided? How can other lawsuits be avoided in the future?

Of course, you have no control over your doctor's level of performance, competence, or efforts to keep up with advancing medical knowledge. But the choice of the doctor who treats you is entirely yours, and the option of consenting to treatment is also yours. You understand full well that taking your child for immunization is a means of preventing some future illness. You are also aware that some modification of your diet, such as limiting calories and cholesterol, along with weight reduction (if appropriate), and exercise, are means of reducing the risk of heart attacks. Infection with measles or polio is neither your fault nor your doctor's fault, but you accept the fact that you, the patient, can take steps to minimize the risk. Likewise, a heart attack is not your "fault," but you, the patient, can take certain steps to decrease the chances of having one.

Let us now examine some ways in which you might reduce the risks of becoming a plaintiff in a malpractice suit, or in other words, reduce the risk of being the victim of an act of negligence, lack of consent, or general dissatisfaction with the care rendered by your doctor.

SPEAK YOUR MIND—AND LISTEN

Open, frank communication between doctor and patient is as effective in heading off serious trouble as it is between husband and wife or between worker and boss. The critical factor is not *agreement* but *communication*. If what you have read in magazines and books leads you to believe that the treatment proposed by your doctor is not the best for you, or the latest available, communicate your doubts. If your doctor is truly empathetic, he will respect your doubts rather than resent them. But don't forget that there is a good chance that *he* might be right and *you* may be wrong or misinformed.

You have the right to expect an explanation of why your doctor selected a particular treatment, or why the one you suggested may not be appropriate to your individual case. Remember that the information *you* have is very generalized, but your doctor's decisions must be based on specific considerations, on the unique circumstances of *your* body and medical history, a body and medical history that are different from all others. As I've mentioned before, such specific information is rarely available to the public, and its application requires the most skillful professional judgment, which is acquired only through extensive training and experience. Perhaps some other medication you habitually take or require will interfere with the action of the drug *you* suggested, and that is why your doctor chose another instead. Perhaps the new wonder drug you heard about on TV is so new that your doctor is still unconvinced of its safety or effectiveness. Perhaps the miraculous cure you read about in the newspaper is still in its experimental stages. Journalists' reports tend to make every new discovery sound like a heavenly gift to medicine, but usually fail to appreciate or mention that many years of experimentation and trial may be necessary before medical experts are convinced that the drug really works or that it is safe and doesn't create a bigger problem than it cures. Furthermore, if the treatment is truly a new drug in the sense of the law, it may not yet be available to your physician. The Food and Drug Administration may have approved it only for special trial programs with a limited number of doctors. As we'll see in Chapter 11, government regulation is weighted in favor of protecting the public from the harmful effects of drugs released for general use before their potential harm is recognized.

WHEN IN DOUBT, MEDIATE

If a frank exchange of ideas between you and your doctor has still left you with some doubts about his or her advice, knowledge, or competence, what are your options?

The most sensible and accessible one is to seek a second opinion (or is it a *third*? We already have your doctor's opinion and *yours*). This should be another professional opinion, not the advice of your neighbor, best friend, golf partner, or mother-in-law. Even the great prophet of health-care services Blue Cross/Blue Shield has finally admitted that a second opinion has value, having so indicated by agreeing to pay the costs of a second opinion before surgery.

The world is made up of people who purchase solid,

heavy, safe motor vehicles for bodily protection, and people who purchase sleek, small, lightweight sports cars despite their deplorable record of not adequately protecting their occupants in a collision. The medical profession, too, has its conservatives and its go-for-broke radicals. An equally competent, knowledgeable, and sincere doctor may choose a more conservative approach to your condition, temporarily at least, in preference to more drastic therapy. Or the second doctor may agree that procrastination can only result in further progression of the condition and eventually greater harm to you. You have no sound basis for making an educated guess at his evaluation in advance, but you can insist on hearing the evaluation before giving your consent.

A word of clarification is required at this point. There are many patients who confuse the quest for a "second opinion" with a search for *agreement*. They have a predetermined and fixed idea of what the diagnosis really is or what the treatment should be, and will go from doctor to doctor until they find one who agrees with them. This is not only very costly, but very foolish. By the time you have heard two opinions that coincide, a third, a fourth, and so on is unlikely to add anything but expense. When you do finally find the oddball physician who agrees with your own idea (and if you look long enough and hard enough, you will most assuredly find one who does), you have spent a lot of money (yours or someone else's, it doesn't really matter), you have allowed your illness to progress without treatment, and you may have placed yourself in the hands of an incompetent doctor, or even a charlatan.

Once upon a time, in days long since gone, an individual doctor may well have discovered a remarkable new treatment that no one else knew about, and patients came from far and near to take the cure. But such a situation is an almost inconceivable idea in today's world. Researchers at the forefront of medical advances fall all over themselves to get into print with their new ideas or concepts, publishing articles in medical journals, making presentations at medical meetings, and writing books. Their fame and fortune is based on telling the world about their innovative thinking, not keeping it secret. The chance of some individual doctor, somewhere, knowing something special that no other doctor is aware of is almost nil. And if such a situation should come to your attention, you should seriously wonder if this marvelous new treatment has been proven safe and effective.

One exception to this rule exists, however. Sometimes a surgeon develops a novel operative technique, and is much more experienced at it than other surgeons. But in such cases, your own doctor may refer you to the specialist surgeon long before you have ever heard of the surgeon's new technique.

In any new drug research program, the government also requires a kind of second opinion, in that similar results must be obtained from at least two or more research centers or doctors before the results can be considered suggestive of valid proof. More commonly, a new drug or treatment has been used successfully by ten, twenty, perhaps fifty different experiment centers before it is considered safe and effective and approved for general use.

A second opinion can be most valuable, even if it agrees totally with the first one. At least it has, or should have, diminished your doubts about the wisdom of proceeding with the treatment first proposed by your doctor.

WHEN TO GRANT CONSENT

The doctrine of *informed consent* as understood in present times dictates that a patient has given consent only when he or she has been fully informed about and *understands* the illness, the proposed treatment, the likelihood of success or failure, and the possible harmful side effects. When you are confident that you have been told the whole story about your proposed treatment, that you have heard a second opinion if you desired it, that you are willing to take the risks of treatment in preference to the risks of nontreatment or more conservative management, only then should you grant permission to proceed by affixing your signature to a consent form. If you grant consent first, then have doubts or dissatisfactions later, you have destroyed much of your legal right to complain about any disappointing results. Your doctor can prove your consent by presenting the complete written document that you signed; by presenting a witness who heard the doctor describe fully to you the possible consequences, good and bad, of treatment and nontreatment, and who observed you agree to and sign the consent form; or by any other means that might convince a judge or jury that you did accept the risks and have no right to complain after the fact. I know of doctors who *tape record* the conversation of informing and consenting, being sure to mention the patient by name and the date, as incontrovertible proof that the discussion did take place and was as complete as it should have been. You may be embarrassed, to say the least, to be presented with such a recording in court while you are testifying that "my doctor never told me."

Of course, not every side effect or unsatisfactory result can be predicted, but if the side effect or result is not predictable, then its occurrence is also not malpractice or negligence.

If you have sought out a research-minded physician in a great medical center who agrees to administer some new, experimental, as-yet-unproven medication, the law *requires* that informed consent be obtained. When the application for approval of the drug is later submitted to the government, proof that informed consent was obtained from every patient must be available for the FDA's inspection. Unlike twenty or more years ago, you can no longer be an unknowing or unwilling participant in an investigational trial. If the trial is to be double-blind, you must be advised of, and you must consent to, the possibility that you might, by random chance, receive the placebo, and in effect be receiving no treatment at all. Of course, you may always withdraw your consent at a later date if you feel you are not getting better. Since there is one chance in two or three that you are receiving no real medication, you will be dropped from the experiment and given a known effective treatment instead. The choice is, and remains, yours exclusively, and investigators are warned against the use of coercion or deception to obtain consent. Obviously such consent is no consent at all under the law.

Inform yourself first, then consent when you are ready. Do not complain afterward that "you didn't know *this* could happen!" unless you or your lawyer discover that the particular side effect was well known and common, and that you should have been, but were not, told of it in advance.

YOUR FAMILY PHYSICIAN

Today's Family Physician is not to be confused with the old G.P. of another era. Family Physicians are highly trained, dedicated doctors who have elected to practice a special kind of medicine that deals with the grand concepts of total family care rather than the intricacies of specific diseases or body systems. Such a physician has probably had two or three years of residency training in a hospital-based Family Practice program after graduation from medical school. He or she may be "Board Certified" in Family Practice, an accomplishment you can identify by the term "Diplomate, American Board of Family Practice" printed on your doctor's letterhead, or the letters "D, ABFP" after his or her name on prescription blanks, business cards, and billheads. The doctor is undoubtedly a member of the American Academy of Family Physicians, may also have been accorded the special honor of being called "Fellow" in the

Academy ("FAAFP"), and strives for recognition as a *specialist in family medicine.*

The American Academy of Family Physicians is a national professional organization with state and county component chapters. It was formed in the late 1940s to assist in maintaining the respect and professional status of the family doctor in the face of the oncoming era of specialist-oriented medicine. To be elected to membership, a doctor must have been in practice at least three years, and must have accumulated at least 150 hours of postgraduate educational credits during that period. Membership is for three years only, and must be renewed by providing proof of 150 additional educational credit hours each time. This group was the first professional organization to require *continuing* education for membership renewal, and as such, set the standard for professional organizations in other specialties later to enact similar requirements. Corresponding requirements are only now being considered for lawyers.

To be elected a Fellow of the Academy (FAAFP) is a further accomplishment, reflecting a more profound participation in continuing medical education.

The American Board of Family Practice was established more recently to provide a means by which family doctors might demonstrate their competence in a manner similar to internists, surgeons, pediatricians, and other specialists. Once again, only this board, which is neither affiliated with nor controlled by the Academy, grants certification, which expires after a finite period of time and must be renewed by reexamination every six years.

The Family Physician is trained to deal with common illnesses, to be aware of the possibility of exotic or rare ones, and to understand the functioning of the whole person and the family unit as it affects the individual's health. The Family Physician is the doctor you are most likely to reach outside of regular office hours, and may well be the most qualified to treat simple, everyday illnesses toward which a specialist may display a patronizing or superior attitude. By the way, the Family Physician also practices during the day! I once received a telephone call at three A.M. from someone I did not know who apologized for calling me at that hour by explaining that "her pediatrician didn't like to be woken up at night." I did get up and see her sick child, but not before asking who had told her that *I* liked being "woken up" at night!

A vital part of the Family Physician's training and expertise is to recognize when his or her knowledge, spread over the vast world of medicine, has reached its limit, when the welfare of the patient demands consultation with or referral to a specialist for diagnosis and/or treatment of the condition.

DO YOU NEED A SPECIALIST?

Today, the Board-Certified specialist in internal medicine also functions as a "primary care" doctor, the one who sees you first and may refer you to a specialist in another field when appropriate. Such doctors list the abbreviation FACP after their name and degree, which stands for "Fellow, American College of Physicians." The use of the term *physician* here is not meant to imply that other doctors are not considered physicians, but rather dates back to a time when only two types of medical doctors were recognized, and the word was used to distinguish the doctor who treated primarily with medications from the one who advocated surgical intervention. The American College of Physicians and the American College of Surgeons were once the only groups of Board-Certified specialists, and were only later joined by other colleges in obstetrics and gynecology, pediatrics, dermatology, and so on.

The specialist, as was noted earlier, has undergone quite a few years of restricted training in a particular field to the exclusion of other areas of medicine. The pediatrician concentrates on diseases of children; the neurologist, on diseases affecting the brain, spinal cord, and nerves (but not "nervous" diseases, more properly called emotional illnesses, which belong in the province of the psychiatrist). If your symptoms *appear* to relate to his area of expertise, but later turn out to be a disease of some other body system, his expertise in this "other" area is probably less than that of the family doctor whose training was much broader. Within his field, of course, he is the expert. The specialist may assist the Family Physician in diagnosing or managing the case through "consultations," may take over its management completely, or may see you first without the prior intervention of the Family Physician or internist. If a specialist's first remark is "What dummy has been taking care of you?" find another specialist quickly. Some doctors seem to feel that their first task is to discredit all prior physicians on the case, implying that they alone are competent. Some delightfully interesting malpractice cases have come to court because the answer to that very stupid question was "Why, your partner, Doctor, last week when you were on vacation."

If you honestly feel that your condition is beyond the competence of your doctor, or if, despite unsuccessful early efforts he or she doesn't seem to want to admit defeat, ask for a reference to a specialist for a consultation. If your doctor refuses, go anyway. A competent Family Physician with a secure professional self-image and a moderate Deity Complex will not object or feel slighted or offended by such a suggestion, and will welcome the opportunity for expert assistance. Sometimes your doctor will suggest it before you do. Your doctor's reaction to the suggestion will tell you a great deal about him. If your welfare is his prime concern, and it certainly should be, he will be pleased either to have the support of an expert who concurs with his diagnosis and treatment or to have a specialist find the true cause of your illness, which was eluding him. The consultation with the specialist is simply another type of second opinion, and we have already discussed the value of getting one. Your eventual choice of the doctor to manage the treatment may be based as much on your own doctor's attitude toward your suggestion of a consultation as it is on your impression of the specialist to whom you are referred. The danger lies in *automatically assuming* that the specialist is better qualified in all situations. He is not, but rather is just an expert in one narrow field.

Frankly, I would not choose to spend five days in the hospital, and have $750 worth of diagnostic tests done on me in order to conclude that I had *had* (by this time it may have spontaneously resolved itself) a simple case of viral gastroenteritis. The Family Physician might have known that 2,600 cases of the illness had been seen in the community in the preceding three weeks, of which he or she had diagnosed 400.

An old professor of mine, listening to us young doctors-in-training discussing the possibility of rare and exotic diseases (to show off our knowledge) in every case on the ward, liked to remind us that "if you hear the sound of hoofbeats downtown in a big city, your first thought should be that it is most likely to be a *horse*. You don't think first of a *zebra!*" While we all like to think that our own illness or condition is unique, and the more neurotic among us *insist* that it is not only rare, but probably serious as well, the simple fact remains that rare and exotic diseases are just that: *rare*. When your new car begins to lose its pep after fifteen thousand miles, your first thoughts are (or should be) directed toward such simple everyday things as a tune-up, new air filter, or new spark plugs, not some rarely heard of defect requiring a whole new power plant. The same applies in medical diagnosis. Those specialists who have been trained to recognize the rare and exotic disease tend to look for them more readily, and sometimes they forget to consider the simpler conditions first.

Make your choice between Family Physician and specialist, then trust in him. If you later begin to think your doctor is an inept fool, remember who made the selection in the first place.

The generalist and the specialist both have a role in the world of medicine. Use both wisely, and they will serve you well.

WHEN YOU CANNOT RESOLVE THE DISAGREEMENT

If, despite repeated attempts you cannot make the doctor understand your reluctance to follow his advice, a second opinion has been of no help in the dispute, and you still cannot come to a meeting of the minds, your choices are limited. But suing the doctor need not be the next logical step. Long before you even think of suing, you can:

1. Change doctors.
2. Demand that your doctor listen to you, or even make a veiled hint of legal action. Sometimes, it is hard to break through, but if you still want to keep him as your doctor, it is worth a try to get him to understand why, for example, you want to take the chance of treating your breast lump with chemotherapy or radiation therapy or both rather than have a radical mastectomy. It is your doctor's obligation to give the best advice, but also to understand your reasoning. If he cannot accept your choice with a clear conscience, he should graciously withdraw from the case and insist that you place yourself in the hands of another doctor. He knows what training and experience have taught him, but cannot know what is in your heart.
3. Seek a second, or even a third (but no more!) opinion on your own, and confront your doctor with them. But if this is your only dispute with him, be gentle about the confrontation. Why is it that only the Orientals fully understand the importance of "saving face"?

CHAPTER 7

THE DOCTOR'S POINT OF VIEW

This chapter is about the professionally competent, sincere doctor who has unwittingly and unwillingly committed an act of malpractice on a patient.

Little sympathy is due the truly incompetent physician or the one who doesn't care for a patient's welfare. It is certainly not my purpose to whitewash the malpractice situation in favor of the medical profession, or to excuse every proper or improper act that a physician may commit. I also do not subscribe to the conspiracy of silence, real or imagined, that is supposed to exist within the medical profession and to some extent, within the legal profession as well. The degree to which lawyers will close ranks to protect *their* colleagues against outside attacks is yet to be measured, for legal malpractice is an infant field, just beginning to be noticed.

THE EMOTIONAL EFFECT OF A
MALPRACTICE SUIT

No one likes to be slapped in the face, or to hear public criticism of his or her faults. "Don't wash the family laundry in public," we were taught as youngsters. The harder one has labored to achieve a satisfactory work performance, the less one wants one's mistakes to be publicly displayed. The more pride one takes in a profession or job, the more an error and its public revelation wound. And finally, the more the error is publicized, the more emotional and defensive the individual becomes.

The average doctor reacts even more poorly to a malpractice suit than do most people upon learning that they have been named as the defendant in a lawsuit. The malpractice suit itself immediately increases anxiety by the florid and lengthy dissertations on general incompetence—of having "misrepresented himself as a qualified physician," and of being unfit overall to practice medicine—that are often incorporated into the complaint. (This is the legal term for the suit that is filed with the court and served on the doctor to initiate the legal proceedings in a malpractice case.) These charges are traditionally included in the complaint in addition to the specific allegations of negligence that form the basis of the suit. Generally they are successful in accomplishing their purpose: to create an emotional reaction, anxiety, and hostility on the part of the defendant doctor. Not being trained to read the factual matters loosely camouflaged in the legal jargon, a doctor reads such a complaint as a personal attack on his or her own integrity rather than a legal "cause of action" for the specific act allegedly committed.

Some lawyers intentionally prepare the written suit in this manner, making it sound as threatening as possible, as a tactical move to inspire thoughts of quick settlement. More likely, however, the worse the allegations sound, the more the doctor resolves to "fight them to the finish." Such points of view are not uncommon in our country, and date back to the eighteenth century and Charles Pinckney's famous outburst to the French government: "Millions for defense but not one penny for tribute." Neither the action nor the reaction is especially reasonable, and the lawyers for both sides are obliged to work to a more objective confrontation. But what is happening in the meantime?

As the doctor's initial anger diminishes and he begins to reflect on the events that led to this predicament, the moment arrives when the doctor must question whether some action, perhaps not as bad as the lawsuit alleges but not as good as was desirable, has triggered the patient to sue. In addition to a list of unflattering thoughts about the patient and the patient's attorney, down deep somewhere there must exist a hint of doubt in any sincere doctor's mind that a different action or method of treatment might have achieved a better result and avoided the lawsuit.

Now this is not to imply that every malpractice suit is based on an actual act of malpractice, or that every doctor is guilty of malpractice just because an accusation has been made. Remember, the HEW study revealed that lawyers themselves feel there is little or no evidence of malpractice in more than half of the cases they accept and prosecute or defend. Some doctors have probably never allowed their judgments to be questioned by anyone throughout their professional lives, but they are few in number. Most suffer inwardly at any mistaken diagnosis or treatment failure. Whether they are sued or not, the satisfaction they seek from the practice of their profession can hardly be found among their failures.

It is not at all uncommon to find the doctor who has recently been named defendant in a malpractice suit or whose trial is imminent becoming preoccupied, anxious, tense, even depressed. This doctor's professional self-image has been seriously compromised, a situation that can hardly be beneficial to his care of other patients, or to a personal life that under the best of circumstances is sorely tried by the demands of a medical practice. Such a doctor wonders why this profession alone among the many in the world is so subject to criticism, second-guessing, and lawsuits, and may wonder how much envy of a substantial income has contributed to the patient's decision to file the suit. To what extent has an attorney's urging been responsible for the suit (less than is commonly believed by the medical profession, as we have already noted)?

What I have learned from speaking with defendant doctors is that suing a doctor has a profound effect on him or her and is not an act that should be taken as lightly as suing a merchant whose goods are defective or a contractor whose work is unsatisfactory. Of course, any patient who has been wronged, injured, abandoned, or neglected or has in any way been the recipient of less than the best effort the doctor was capable of making deserves compensation in one form or another, deserves a day in court if that is the only alternative left. But just as the careless doctor must be made to see the error of his ways, the potential plaintiff patient must know the effects any lawsuit will have on the physician. Emotionally, the effects can be severe.

THE FINANCIAL EFFECTS OF A MALPRACTICE SUIT

With barely a microcosm of exceptions, no physician today practices without professional liability insurance to cover financial loss from malpractice suits, whether meritorious or frivolous, including those settled quickly for small sums of money on the basis of "nuisance value" (i.e., it will cost more and be far more trouble to defend even a wholly defensible case than to pay the small compensation sought or suggested at the pretrial hearing). The amount of insurance protection a physician purchases relates primarily to the

anticipated size of court awards prevalent at the time, much
as you would tailor your own homeowners' or automobile
liability insurance to the economic nature of your community or the luxuriousness of your car and the likely maximum claim against you. Obviously a single award several
hundred thousand dollars above the insurance coverage
would wipe out most people, doctors included. Unless they
are heirs to a large inheritance or have made a most fortu-
nate investment, doctors by and large are not nearly as
wealthy as most of their patients think they are. I recall a
patient who strolled into my office in the third month of
my first year in practice and told the receptionist (my wife
—I could not yet afford hired help) that she had the patient
to thank for her mink coat. We couldn't decide whether
to laugh, cry, or get angry; we were still wondering how to
make the payments on the house-office, the equipment and
furnishings in the office (considerably more than we had
upstairs in the living area), and the used car.

Nevertheless, it is highly unlikely that anything short of
an exceptional and extraordinary award by the court will
personally cost the doctor anything at all, at least not for
the moment, and not *directly*.

But let's look a bit further into the money world we are
discussing. What other economic effects will a malpractice
suit have? *Someone* has to pay the award if the suit is lost,
and the costs of defending it even when the doctor wins.
The insurance carrier will not pay the costs without reacting
in some fashion, most likely by raising malpractice insurance premiums for the following year based on "claims-paid
experience." The premiums will go up not just to the doctor
defendant in this case, but for all doctors insured by that
carrier, and especially all doctors in the same specialty. A
more drastic move, seen with ever-increasing frequency in
the late seventies and early eighties, is for the insurance
company to conclude that the malpractice insurance business isn't profitable enough and withdraw from participa-

tion in that state, or withdraw from it entirely, leaving large groups of doctors scrambling for substitute coverage, inevitably at a far higher rate.

Malpractice insurance premiums, which are based on both the state or locale of practice and the type of practice, recently ranged from a low of about $1,000 per year for certain very low risk specialties in rural areas of the South to a high of $75,000 *per year* or more! Annual increases of between 50 and 200 percent are not at all uncommon. And these figures relate to the lower levels of protection. Some doctors carry astronomical amounts of protection "just in case." By way of comparison, we consumers worry about 10 percent increases in the cost of food, clothing, or automobiles, and are horrified by 25 percent increases in the price of gasoline.

But who eventually *really* pays for the increase in premiums? The same person who pays for government-mandated pollution-control devices on cars, or the increased costs of manufacturing after a strike-induced rise in salaries: you, the consumer, the buyer, the user of medical services. No business, not even a medical practice, however altruistic a doctor might be, can operate indefinitely at a loss. If insurance is to cost the doctor $10,000, $20,000, $75,000 a year, then his fees must be sufficient to cover it along with other expenses such as office rent, equipment with which to serve you, salaries for a nurse and receptionist, billing costs, and so on, and still leave a profit.

The medical profession is acutely aware of the malpractice situation, and feels obliged to practice what has been termed "defensive medicine." This does not mean that the doctor incurs expenses or performs certain acts to "cover up," Watergate-style, any errors or inadequacies. What it does mean is that doctors now tend to order extra laboratory tests, extra X rays, more sophisticated tests, extra days in the hospital, or extra office follow-ups for the primary purpose of documenting the accuracy and correctness of their diagnosis and treatment, and to prove the nonexistence of other illnesses that their clinical judgment had already indicated were probably not present. Clinical judgment alone, however, is not an adequate defense in a lawsuit. Expert witnesses will readily testify with the benefit of hindsight that the doctor "should have discovered" some other condition that developed later or that may have been present but was as yet undetectable at the time of examination. Only by protecting his flanks can your doctor guard against lawsuits of questionable justification that may nonetheless be successful in a courtroom. And who pays for *these* additional costs? *You* do, directly or via your health insurance carrier, who raises premiums, or the government agency, which in turn raises the taxes that pay for a program such as Medicare.

The legal profession and consumer advocates deny this accusation, maintaining instead that sophisticated tests are necessary for the welfare of the patient. They are—sometimes. But a doctor's clinical judgment is still the finest diagnostic tool available, and a competent, knowledgeable doctor's judgment is usually confirmed, rarely reversed, by the "extra" testing done for defensive reasons, as contrasted with tests necessary to confirm an initial diagnosis or quantitatively measure the degree of disease present.

Such are the financial effects of a malpractice suit. Little financial hardship is inflicted directly on the doctor–defendant. Much hardship is inflicted on the profession as a whole, and by extension, on the consumer of health services. If such services are paid for by an employer, a union, or a government agency, the same situation will, *must*, prevail. A government has one primary source of revenue: the taxpayer. A union has one primary source of revenue: the membership. A business may pass on the increased costs of health insurance by reducing its outlay for

annual bonuses or raises, by reducing its annual contribu-
tion to pension funds, and by raising its prices for the goods
or services it provides.

Here, truly, is the malpractice crisis.

HOW A MALPRACTICE SUIT AFFECTS THE PHYSICIAN PROFESSIONALLY

"Where there's smoke, there's fire," mother used to say.
Accusations levied against a physician in a malpractice
action may be "front-page news" or "choice gossip," but
vindication of the doctor is rarely the object of much interest or attention beyond his own family. Physicians whose
malpractice suits have become public knowledge suffer some
harm to their professional reputation whether the suit was
just or frivolous, or merely vengeful. Whether the doctor
finally won or lost rarely makes any difference, or even
comes to the attention of those whose impression of him
has diminished. Moreover, a malpractice suit cannot fail to
have a deleterious effect on the doctor's attitude toward his
patients.

The fear of future malpractice suits may even affect a
doctor's choice of treatment. As a specific example, the
U.S. Department of Health and Human Services found
that obstetricians are now delivering 15 percent of the
nation's babies by Caesarean section and the percentage is
still climbing. Dr. Helen Marieskind, a Seattle health administrator and the author of the study based on a review
of medical literature and interviews with more than 100
obstetricians, found that while many of the Caesarean sec-
tions have valid medical reasons, the most frequent reason
given is a fear that the doctors will be sued if they do not
perform a Caesarean and a "less than perfect infant" is
born. What a poor reason to use to decide on a treatment
method. It is well known and confirmed by Dr. Marieskind's
study that:

1. Claims are more often filed in connection with a surgical birth (Caesarean) than with a normal delivery.
2. Both the rate of complication and the costs of delivery rise significantly when more Caesarean deliveries are performed at the expense of vaginal deliveries.
3. At least one-third of the women undergoing this procedure suffer from postoperative infections and an estimated one in one thousand *die*.
4. There is a high rate of serious respiratory illness among babies born to mothers who previously had delivered by Caesarean.

This illustrates most graphically how the malpractice crisis coupled with a failure to provide full disclosure of risks operates to the detriment of both patient and doctor and benefits neither.

It is easy to take sides, though difficult to substantiate or support your position, on whether the patient or the physician is responsible for the deterioration of the professional relationship. The unfortunate results, however, benefit neither party. Regardless of the cause or the specifics of any particular lawsuit, a lawsuit is a situation in which everyone loses. Respect, once lost, is rarely recovered.

CHAPTER 8

THE RIGHTS OF A HOSPITAL PATIENT

CONFINEMENT, OR INTERNMENT?

When in the course of human events you find yourself requiring hospitalization, you are entering what is perhaps the arena of greatest dispute between the patient and the health-care community. It is also the source of the greatest number of complaints, and undeniably the generator of the largest bills—bills that are astonishing at times even to doctors, on the rare occasions when they see the financial results of their well-intentioned and sometimes defensive care. Few patients understand the mysterious world of the hospital, and few hospital staff members understand the real difference between "the body in 227-A" and you as an individual, human-type creature, someone's mother/father, son/daughter, wife/husband.

A hospital is a large, well- or poorly organized confluence of persons of greater or lesser training and skill, all of whom form a necessary part of an institution that has a single objective: the care of the sick or allegedly sick. It functions in part as a sophisticated diagnostic center, in part as a place in which health care is rendered (tender-loving or otherwise), in part as a teaching center for new entrants into the health-care professions, and in part as a hotel of sorts. The problems inherent in combining all of these functions are extraordinary, and they are not always addressed in the most desirable, most efficient, or most effective manner, though the intent of doing a good job is almost always present in those charged with the responsibility. Yes, I know that from the *patient's* point of view the hospital experience often leaves a great deal to be desired. It does from the doctor's point of view as well, and many nurses and technicians are also frequently left dissatisfied, to say nothing of the maintenance staff. In short, the hospital is a small *world*, fraught with all the failings of humankind, and an almost incredible amount of success. It is not my purpose to excuse the goings-on in hospitals, only to try to help you live with them when it becomes necessary for you to be engulfed by this unique world. No one *wants* to be in a hospital, but at times it becomes more or less necessary, even desirable, for your well-being or even for your survival.

We speak in formal terms of a patient's being "confined" to the hospital for a greater or lesser period of time. Many patients have told me they feel they are in something resembling a prison or concentration camp (some people do like to exaggerate), their own rights and desires are so little acknowledged. This is how I came to title this section "Confinement, or Internment?" It *should* be the former, though it may sometimes seem like the latter.

FOR *WHOSE* CONVENIENCE?

Within the sterile walls of one of these noble institutions rests, at any given moment, a great multitude known to the staff and management as the patient population. Actually, of course, the patients are a number of individual persons with individual likes, dislikes, needs, desires, personalities, and grievance levels, some more accepting, subservient, or cooperative than others, depending on who is doing the defining or the categorizing. However much the hospital as a whole, or individual staff members, may wish or try to address all of these needs *individually*, it becomes necessary for the most part to address all of them *collectively*. What this means is simply that *some* of the needs, desires, wishes, and preferences of the individual patients must be sacrificed knowingly, or even ignored, in deference to the general functioning of the institution so that at least some or most of the needs and wishes of all may be accommodated. Clearly, the function of the hospital as a center for health care takes precedence over its function as a hotel, and consequently the *medical needs* must be given primary importance at the expense of other desires, wishes, and preferences. After all, that you get your medications as ordered, or that your operation or diagnostic tests are carried out when required is certainly more important than whether or not you are fed at the hour you like to eat, or even whether the food is still hot when it arrives at your bedside from the kitchen eleven floors below and three annexes west. It would be nice if the food were hot, delicious, and exactly what you ordered when you filled out today's menu (which they had you do yesterday morning, or three days ago), but such amenities are not critical.

To put aside once and for all the subject of hospital food, it is no better and no worse than any other kind of institutional food, and certainly better than some military messes (that choice of word for military dining facilities always intrigued me). Was there ever a soldier, a college dorm resident, a company cafeteria diner, or a hospital staff member (they don't eat any better than the patients!) who didn't find the culinary fare far from ideal?

Among the most frequently voiced gripes of hospital patients are the "odd" times the patient (to his or her way of thinking) is disturbed for such mundane things as the taking of temperature, pulse, and blood pressure. For some reason the measurement of pulse and blood pressure is considered medically necessary and tolerable, but the taking of one's temperature appears as an unnecessary intrusion on one's privacy, especially in the middle of the night. In partial defense, the nurse is obliged to follow the doctor's orders, and if your doctor wants to know about your temperature at the traditional four-hour intervals, the nurse must measure and record it. Our bodies do not remain at the same temperature throughout the twenty-four-hour day, whether sick or well. Rather, we have a daily cycle that (as parents of young children know perfectly well) places the highest body temperature of the day in late afternoon or early evening—shortly after the doctor's office has closed—and the lowest twelve hours away in the early morning. The full cycle may be important to the doctor. I concede, though, that the doctor who orders "vital signs every four hours" just as a habit is *not* being very considerate of a patient and could, with an extra twitch of the pen, order them "seven A.M. to midnight" or even "if awake." Ask your doctor if such orders can be changed.

Another complaint is the frequency—or lack of same—with which nurses "look in" on the patient. Nurses usually look in more often than most patients realize. The patient may have dozed off, may have been "observed" while out walking the corridor (after all, such observation, too, has a clinical purpose. Some patients can't stand up at all!) or while sitting in the solarium or recreation area, talking with other patients, friends, or relatives, playing cards or reading. Such observations are diligently recorded in the patient's chart by each and every nurse, who runs through many pens in the course of a year. "Awake and alert, no complaints" is a meaningful observation to your doctor. Sometimes these notes read "comatose" or "screaming in pain." Finally, what you may have thought was two nurses chewing the fat as they entered your room for a few seconds was more than likely the thrice-daily shift change and the required patient-by-patient brief visit and report as one shift turns over the responsibility for the ward and the inhabitants to the next. More writing in the chart.

What about all those times when you rang the call bell and "no one came for hours"? Most modern call systems will continue to sound at the nurses' station until someone comes into the patient's room and resets it. Consequently, you will get a response as soon as possible, if for no other reason than to enable someone to turn off the buzzer or beeper. As you lie in bed, uncomfortable and waiting, seconds do seem like hours. Consider how much more important you might consider the delay if your call were for a real emergency, and at times that's precisely what the delay is all about: the entire available nursing staff on the floor is otherwise engaged in handling some emergency while awaiting the hurried arrival of a doctor, or assisting some doctor with an examination or procedure. It is next to impossible, for example, to save the life of a patient who suffers a cardiac arrest unless the nurse(s) on duty in the ward can start CPR (cardiopulmonary resuscitation) immediately while another nurse sounds the alert. Would you seriously give higher priority to your need for a pillow fluff or the bedpan just because you rang first?

Doctors, even the residents who are full-time employees of the hospital and work only there, are responsible for patients throughout the institution, and only by sheer coincidence might they be nearby when an emergency takes place. Just as health-care needs must take precedence over common amenities, emergencies must take precedence over less urgent patient needs.

There are callous nurses who ignore patients. There aren't as many as you may think, but they do exist. Every profession has its misfits and its bad apples. They aggravate the doctors even more than they do the patients. We must depend on them in our absence. But I never saw a nurse voluntarily go to sleep on a cot in or around the nurses' station on the night shift, as I have heard many patients say they do. The night shift, however, *is* one-half or one-quarter the size of the day shift, and this is reflected in how long it may take the night nurses to respond to a call. They suffer from the same lack of talent as the rest of us: no matter how urgent, there is no way for one body to be in two places at the same time.

The same condition holds for the interns and residents, those young men and women who do the thirty-six-hour shifts and are expected to be in *eight* places at once, not two. I have seen "calls" for the doctor recorded by the switchboard operator (never one to be terribly sympathetic toward the young doctors) at, say, 2:45 A.M., and the floor nurse recording his or her arrival in response to a call at 2:54 A.M., only to have the patient file a loud and formal complaint the next morning that it took "hours" to get a doctor to come in and take care of whatever problem precipitated the situation. Asleep on duty? During that part of my life I used to catch twenty winks (not enough time for forty) leaning against the wall in the patient's room while the nurse propped him or her up in bed for me to examine. Those naps were frequently the closest I ever came to sleep during my nights on duty, which were preceded and followed by a full day of work.

When you question why the nurse arrives to take your pulse, blood pressure, and temperature just as you begin to eat your meal, which, for once, arrived reasonably hot, remember that the nurse must go, bed by bed, through the whole ward, and arrives at the last bed quite some time after the first. The kitchen staff follows a similar routine, and if they happen to do the floor in the opposite direction, it is just possible that the two routines collide. A little patience and understanding on your part makes life more pleasant for everyone, especially you.

But we are supposed to be talking about the rights of the patient, and here I am "defending" the hospital. Or am I? What I have been doing is *explaining* why certain inconveniences are a necessary part of hospital routine, not examples of cold-hearted indifference. Most nurses are very sincere in their desire to help, and they do the best they can under trying and difficult circumstances. Many will also go out of their way to *please* insofar as it is possible to do so, and are just as frustrated as the patients when they are unable to succeed.

If your objections are to the procedures or medications the doctor ordered and you complain to the nurse, you only place the nurse in an impossible situation. Forced to choose between accommodating the irritable or unco-operative patient and following the doctor's orders, the nurse *must* do the latter until the doctor modifies or retracts the instructions. It is not a nurse's place to decide whether they are necessary or not; it is the nurse's place to make known your unhappiness to the doctor, either during the doctor's next visit or, if the complaint seems urgent enough, by telephone. At the very least, the nurse will usually make note of the complaint in the chart (some doctors, myself included, diligently read nurses' notes; some never do) and notify the next shift. But only the doctor can change or delete those orders. Presumably they were written for your immediate or remote welfare, not for spite.

An ideal hospital would have one nurse for every patient, or at least one for every double room. Add one nurse's aide and perhaps one "candy-striper" (hospital volunteer, often a teenager) for each couple of rooms, and you might approach the kind of personal attention you feel you deserve as a paying customer, and a sick one at that. A millionaire could buy the hospital, evict all the other patients, and have the whole staff at his beck and call. But the rest of us must share the staff with all the other sick people equally entitled to attention and care, some more, some a bit less, depending on their state of health.

What about those times they took you to the X-ray department and just left you there for an hour before anyone got around to taking your picture? Couldn't they have waited until everything was ready for you? How about the hour and a half you spent, in great anxiety and considerable discomfort, on that hard hospital cart outside of the operating room waiting for your turn for surgery? Surely they could schedule things better than that!

Unfortunately, they can't. They would *like* to, but things do not often go that smoothly, and when they don't, changes in schedule are necessarily unanticipated. For example, if the patient being X-rayed ahead of you is held up because the doctor thinks he sees something and wants another film shot from a different angle, that means a delay. What happens if they don't send for you until the patient before you is completely finished? An orderly must be found to come for you, he must search for an available cart, he arrives at your room to find you in the bathroom, six crowded elevators go by before the orderly can squeeze you and the cart on one, and you finally arrive at the X-ray department, having kept everybody waiting for a long time. You might be spared an hour's wait for your X ray, but the long delays caused by the wait for every patient might mean that your X ray is delayed not just an hour but until the next day.

Each type of surgical procedure is known to take a certain average amount of time, and the successive operations for an operating room are scheduled accordingly. The first operation each morning starts on time. But if the first presents some unforeseen difficulty and takes two hours when the average time was forty-five minutes, operation two starts an hour and a quarter late, and everything goes downhill from there for the rest of the day. The medications given to you in preparation for surgery work on a time schedule, and when your entry into surgery is delayed an hour or two, the delay causes the doctors more problems than it causes you.

Most routines around a hospital may be annoying, but remember that they are being done for your *well-being*, not your convenience. (And not for the doctor's, the nurse's, or the hospital's convenience either!) The operating room nurse and the X-ray technician are even more interested in finishing their work and going home on time than you are in getting back to your room. Are there abuses? Certainly. There always are in every phase of life. But they are the exception.

LINES OF COMMUNICATION AND CHAINS OF COMMAND

Let's assume for the moment, for the sake of argument, that you have a complaint, a perfectly legitimate and justified one. You are angry and frustrated. You dump on the next person who walks into the room with a hospital employee name tag on his or her tunic, blouse, or shirt. Is this the way to handle the problem?

If that "next person" is the nurse assigned to your section of the ward, probably. If it's the candy-striper volunteer, hardly. The volunteer wants for all the world to help you, but if he or she becomes the object of your wrath or abuse, you minimize the chances of receiving such volunteer help again. Who did you help? If your complaint is about cold food, why tell the nurse? Tell the kitchen-staff person who brought it in, and if he or she appears indifferent (and they often do), ask your nurse to have the dietitian visit you. It is the dietitian's job not only to help you get the variety of food that would please you (within the confines of any special diet your doctor has ordered) but to see that the service is up to at least minimum reasonable standards.

On the other side of the coin, I have seen patients vent their anger on the porter who happens to come in with a mop to clean the floor and who, with a glance of astonishment or just plain lack of interest, keeps on working and leaves with total amnesia for anything the patient said. That night the porter will be telling everyone, "You should have heard the nut on the third floor . . ." but you will have accomplished absolutely nothing other than to gain notoriety as a "nut" among the porters and their friends!

Suppose you complain to your nurse(s) and nothing changes. Should you demand to see the administrator, call your Congressman, or send for your lawyer? That's not a reasonable "chain of command." Far more effective is to ask for the head nurse on the floor and explain your problem. The next step up if you are still unsatisfied is the nursing supervisor, who is responsible for several wards in a large hospital or the entire shift of nurses in a small one. If you are still getting nowhere, mention the problem to your doctor the next time he or she visits. Your physician may be able to straighten out the problem or modify orders to accommodate you, or perhaps simply explain why the inconvenience is necessary and is being inflicted on his order. But be reasonable in explaining what it is that is bothering you and why. A general blast about "the incompetent nursing staff" can result in your doctor's ignoring it as an unreasonable collection of complaints from an uncooperative patient, or conversely cause him or her to take your "general blast" and refire it, with the embellishments of a doctor's stature, ego, and Deity Complex, at the "whole nursing staff." This does not endear either you or your doctor to the nurses, and while they will, for the most part, still try to be professional and continue to render proper care, they are also human and could not possibly render the same quantity or quality of tender loving care under those conditions.

Start with the assumption that the hospital staff would really like to do the best it can for you and get rid of you as soon as possible, for "getting rid of you" means that you are feeling better, well enough to be discharged. Don't assume they are all engaged in a widespread conspiracy to make your life miserable. It doesn't work that way. They only get another patient when you leave.

Several years ago there appeared on the cinema screens an award-winning film called *One Flew Over The Cuckoo's Nest*. Among other things, it portrayed a sadistic nurse who got her jollies by tormenting patients. That character became the epitome of hospital nurses for those current or former patients who had had a bad experience in a hospital and now felt supported in their beliefs that such is the stock of which nurses are made. True or false? It *is* true—here and there in an isolated individual, obviously emotionally ill, who *abuses* the profession. But in almost every case, the sadistic stereotype is decidely false. Nurses (and allied hospital professionals) are spread out across the same bell-shaped curve that applies to any group. Most nurses are reasonably competent, reasonably pleasant, and reasonably effective at their jobs. A few are brilliant, exceptional, or extraordinary in their sincere feelings for the sick. Born a generation later, they might have become physicians. A few, down at the bottom end of the curve, are incompetent, lazy, or just plain mean. A sprinkle at the very extreme are sick and don't belong in such a profession—or in any trade or profession where they must deal with people.

In part because we expect so much more of them (the

image of Florence Nightingale), and in part because when we come into contact with them we are ill or injured and almost always frightened and not in our best mood to understand or compromise, we tend to expect the highest level of achievement from each and every person in the health-care community. Life doesn't work out that way. Whether you have two children or ten, one may achieve more than you ever dreamed, and another may be a terrible disappointment to you, the "black sheep" of the family. We are unable to weed out all the truly inappropriate ones from any profession ahead of time, and health-care professionals are no exception. Nor am I for one moment excluding physicians from this hazard. Most are reasonably good—it's rather difficult to get through medical school without some minimum level of intelligence—but a few are brilliant and a few remain less than competent, while a few are indeed mentally ill or dishonest. All applicants must meet certain minimum standards to obtain a driver's license, but some should never have been passed and turned loose on the road.

When voicing your dissatisfactions through a regular and well-established chain of command, the odds are next to nil that you could approach two or three successive levels of incompetent, sick, or unfeeling people. By the second, certainly the third, level, you will have found someone empathetic to your legitimate complaint and willing to either rectify it or at least explain why it is a necessary inconvenience.

I DON'T NEED A SLEEPING PILL; I WAS ALREADY ASLEEP

Unlike the two A.M. thermometer for which there may have been a valid need, I do agree that it makes no sense to awaken a patient in order to administer a sleep aid. Almost always the doctor has ordered it "if needed," and that is one determination that ought to be left to the patient to make, by implication at least.

But such an occurrence is representative of different things that may happen to you in the hospital that may appear to be unreasonable but that are, sometimes, not unreasonable at all. On the other hand, sometimes you are quite right. Sometimes things are done by reason of someone else's judgment when you should have been allowed some say in the matter along the lines of our discussion about informed consent. If you feel you have been denied your right, *don't squawk, talk*—to the appropriate person or persons. Don't complain to the lab technician that you think you are getting too many blood tests. He or she has been sent to draw your blood, not to decide how often, how much, or why. The technician can't change any of the instructions. Think! Who is likely to be responsible for ordering a blood test? Right. Tell your doctor, but don't expect too much sympathy. Doctors aren't vampires, and have no use for your blood other than to have it analyzed for some piece of information they need.

There used to be a single reason for taking an X ray: to visualize something inside the body that could not otherwise be seen without cutting an opening and looking in. Since photography was a great deal less traumatic than surgery, and no real dangers were associated with this specialized kind of photography (or so we *thought*), it was considered a great boon to the practice of medicine, and Dr. Wilhelm Roentgen, who discovered X rays, was accorded great honors. In fact, "roentgenography" is the official name by which we know the procedure. The term X *ray* connotes the mysterious, "science-fiction" kind of awe in which we held so marvelous an innovation in its early days.

In these enlightened days of consumer awareness, environmental protection, and "no nukes," we have modified our thinking somewhat in line with the knowledge that too much radiation of any kind can be harmful. (It is, of course, the X rays that cause the problem, not the *film*.) There are now two reasons for taking X rays:

1. To visualize something inside the body that could not otherwise be seen, with or without computer enhancement
2. To document for the record the absence of some condition or disease the doctor knows isn't there but could be called upon someday to prove, should the disease develop at a later date and the patient later sue

Finally, we have become sufficiently educated to understand that those invisible rays are cumulative during an individual's lifetime and if the sum total is sufficient, can be deadly. Does this mean you should object strenuously, refuse consent, and threaten to sue every time someone suggests a visit to the radiology department? Of course not.

You have no way of knowing where the line is drawn between the X rays ordered for reason one and those ordered for reason two, but you can ask—only don't ask the X-ray technician. His or her job is to know how to position you and the film carrier and the machine for the best visualization of whatever it is the doctor wants to see, and to determine the appropriate "exposure" for a good film. They used to also have to know how to develop the films but another machine usually does that automatically these days. Obviously the technician has no idea beyond speculation as to *why* the doctor ordered the films, and certainly has no authority to take any more or less of them than ordered.

Once again the person to query is the one who ordered the X rays in the first place: your doctor. It's not necessary (or even prudent or polite) to confront him with an accusation of taking too many X rays for purely defensive purposes, bombarding you with radiation for *his* benefit, not yours. But you *can* inquire if your doctor already has a reasonably certain diagnosis, and what chances he really thinks there may be that some other, up-to-now obscure, disease exists that may only be revealed by more pictures. Then, armed with these answers, decide whether you wish to heed the advice that another set of films is really in your best interests. Together, cognizant of your concern about radiation, you may decide to postpone another group of X rays until such time as they seem really necessary for some bona fide medical reason. Among these might be confirmation of a suspected additional diagnosis, discovery of an otherwise undetectable condition, or visualization of results or progress of treatment, such as regression of a tumor or ulcer or healing of a fracture.

Sometimes it seems necessary for doctors to order multiple series of X rays for a combination of the two reasons given earlier. Thus a chronic abdominal condition might cause a doctor to order, in rapid succession, an upper G.I. series (visualizing the stomach and small intestine, usually done when an ulcer is suspected), a barium enema to visualize the large intestine (colon) and rectum in search of cancer, diverticulitis, or a few other conditions, and a gall bladder series to spot gallstones. In most cases a careful history (medical interview and review of symptoms) and a physical examination would probably have revealed that the most likely diagnosis was in only one of these three areas, and necessitated only one of the three series of films. This is a very general discussion, and not meant to second-guess *your* doctor about *your* situation. In some specific instances, there might be very good reason to do all three and even some others, but like the sleeping pill, the question is "Do you need it?"

I say only that X rays, like all tests and medical procedures, should be done for a reason, not for the lack of a reason not to, and certainly not in place of the careful history and physical examination. I am opposed to that kind of medical practice and consider it lazy and irresponsible. It is, unfortunately, gradually becoming more common, and at least part of the blame must rest with the patients and the increasing number and extent of and reasons for malpractice suits, and the steps the doctor consequently feels must be taken for his own protection. Sometimes your doctor ceases to be concerned with whether these steps are potentially harmful or expensive to you, reasoning that these are *your* problems, since you are the cause of having to do them. Mutual distrust again, and everyone is hurt.

Do not misinterpret this discussion to imply that all or most doctors order unnecessary X rays willy-nilly. The medical profession has expended great efforts to find alternative ways of visualizing internal structures without the use of radiation whenever possible. Among these are the relatively new techniques such as ultrasound, a kind of sonar procedure believed to be harmless even to so delicate an object as an unborn fetus. Where ultrasound is not feasible, X-ray equipment and techniques have been developed that permit X-ray like films that require a much lower exposure to the rays themselves. In this category we find computerized axial tomography (CAT scans), other computer-enhanced X-ray techniques, and new ultrasensitive plates and films that can record the same quality image with but a tiny fraction of the exposure, similar to high-speed photographic films for your camera that can make an acceptable picture in low light without flash.

The message is—again—the same old one: communicate. If you have doubts, if you are unhappy, if you have strong feelings about radiation, talk about them rationally with your doctor. The most foolish and counterproductive approach of all in such a situation is to put up with your undesired treatment, take the consequences (additional radiation), and then sue the doctor if something goes wrong. Even if you win money, and the chances are heavily against it, you cannot deduct from your body the "rems" (the unit by which we measure radiation) you have accumulated.

I CAN OBJECT, BUT DO I HAVE *RIGHTS*?

Recognizing the problems we have been discussing and hopeful of initiating some effort to overcome them, the American Hospital Association has proposed "A Patient's Bill of Rights." While the document has no official authority, it is nominally subscribed to by the hospitals that are members of the association, and that means most of the hospitals in the country. The Bill of Rights contains twelve points, which are summarized below. They have been incorporated in their entirety in at least one bill under consideration by a state legislative body, Assembly Bill No. 464, State of New Jersey, 1982. A copy of the full proposed law may be found in the Appendices.

A Patient's Bill of Rights states that a patient has a right:

1. To considerate and respectful care
2. To receive complete current information about diagnosis, treatment, and prognosis
3. To receive that information necessary to enable him to grant informed consent
4. To refuse treatment and to be informed of the medical consequences
5. To consideration of confidentiality about his or her treatment
6. To expect that the hospital will hold in confidence all records of his treatment
7. To expect the hospital to make a reasonable response to his requests for services
8. To obtain information about any relationship of the hospital with other health-care and educational institutions where it might relate to his care

9. To be advised if the hospital plans to use him in human experimentation programs and to refuse to participate in such projects
10. To expect continuity of care
11. To examine and receive an explanation of his bill
12. To know what hospital rules and regulations apply to his conduct as a patient

This Bill of Rights does not, as yet, have the authority of law, but it's a start.

CHAPTER 9

THE RIGHTS OF AN OFFICE PATIENT

THE FOLLY OF BEING AN ADVERSARY

The recurrent theme throughout this book has been a simple one: You go to a doctor because you feel ill and would like to feel better. The doctor is not perfect and neither are you. Nevertheless, in order to achieve your goal of feeling better, it stands to reason that the approach most likely to succeed is one in which, initially at least, both of you enter the relationship with some modicum of trust and belief that the outcome will be good and that, at the very minimum, you will feel better than you did when you arrived. After all, you don't really need either the doctor or the bill to make you feel worse. (You can probably do that on your own at little or no cost.) No, what you seek from the doctor is a step forward and upward. What he or she seeks from you is some combination of satisfaction at doing a job well, and income, the ratio of

122

the two being different for each doctor and possibly even for each patient he or she takes on. Some cases are so challenging to a doctor's intellect, or so apparently hopeless at first sight, that a favorable outcome is remarkably satisfying to both of you and the fee is very secondary. No fee can equal the sense of elation at having revived a dead patient by properly applied CPR quickly enough to prevent brain damage. Other cases are so routine, dull, or even annoying that the fee is a primary motivation. Both reactions are very human.

The one situation that never made any sense at all to me was the one in which either the doctor or the patient or both fervently wished they had never met each other while they were still engaged in the doctor–patient relationship. It happens occasionally to every doctor and to most patients. When it happened to me, I would tell the patient, as diplomatically as I could, that continuing the relationship made no sense, that I couldn't be of help so long as he or she distrusted everything I said and did, and that instead of continuing to come to my office and causing considerable aggravation to *both* of us, it would be far better to find another, more satisfying physician. I explained that we would part without bitterness or anger if at all possible, that I would provide any new doctor with a complete summary of the patient's records and the results of all laboratory tests done in the recent past to avoid costly and unnecessary repetition, and would cooperate in any way possible to help the new doctor establish a better relationship than the one I had with this patient. Sometimes it made for a better understanding between us; if nothing else, it removed a thorn from both of our sides.

Your body is not like your car. If you distrust your mechanic without cause, he may still be able to tune up your engine competently or replace your brake linings properly. Not so with your body, however. Our minds are too intimately connected to and associated with our body functions. So long as you *believe* your doctor is not doing an effective job in caring for your symptoms or disease, they will not go away. In fact, you may develop new ones, "proof" that your doctor is incompetent, although in reality you are only experiencing psychosomatic (*psycho* means "mind," not "crazy"; *soma* means "body") effects of your mental dissatisfaction. Unhappy spouses, frustrated employees, and overly stressed children develop all kinds of symptoms, some quite bizarre and some mimicking known disease conditions.

I am making a pitch for evaluating your relationship with your doctor and your estimate of the quality of your doctor's care as it progresses, and if it falls short of your expectations, of *terminating* it before it results in something awful happening to you. You have obligations to the doctor (to pay him so long as you use his services), and he has several to you (to render care that is up to the accepted standard, not to abandon you in midstream, to act in your best interests, to obtain informed consent before doing anything to you, and so on), but nowhere is there an obligation on either party, real, imagined, or implied, to *continue* an unsatisfactory union beyond the point at which one or both of you would really rather end it. We Americans are a proud and independent people. If you don't care for your doctor or the way he is taking care of you, move on.

THE DOCTOR'S ADVICE VERSUS THE NURSE'S ADVICE

I'm not sure whether the fault is greater on the part of the patients or on those surrounding the doctor and involved in his or her relationships with patients. It's probably spread around equally. But patients do have a tendency to consider everyone associated with the doctor as qualified to speak on his or her behalf, and the doctor's staff in turn feel perfectly confident in doing so, oblivious of the fact that they lack the doctor's extensive education and experience. Sometimes they have no medical background at all.

Nurses, receptionists, pharmacists, and other such "nearly medical" persons do not and cannot acquire the same quantity and quality of knowledge as that which results from ten or fifteen years of intensive education and on-the-job training, to say nothing of the years or decades of hands-on practical experience. No matter how often they observe the physician at work or see the end results of his or her thinking (e.g., prescriptions), only a smattering of the doctor's knowledge is ever acquired. If they have been "hanging around" an incompetent physician, the incompetence is now exponentially multiplied.

Economics, regrettably, comes into play in this situation. If you visit the doctor—occasionally even if you only consult by phone—you know you will be charged a fee. If you extract some tidbit of information from a nurse or receptionist and/or "consult" with the pharmacist, you also know that it is free advice. All true—and so is the old adage that "you get what you pay for." Sometimes you get less than you pay for, but it is highly unlikely that you will ever get *more* than you pay for.

I don't want to leave you with the impression—it would be an inaccurate one—that I am "putting down" the nursing or pharmacy professions. Both contain learned professionals, who know their business well if they are competent. There are things, pertinent to *their* professions, which they know *better* than a physician, but medical diagnosis and medical treatment rightfully belongs in a *doctor's* bailiwick, and it is the physician who is the expert on these matters. Many pharmacists know more about certain aspects of the use of therapeutic medications than some of their physician friends, but when they venture into the area of diagnosis by reason of a small conversation with you at the prescription counter and pretend to come to a better conclusion than a doctor who has had the benefit of a history-taking session, a physical examination, and a multitude of tests, they have wandered well beyond their "learned profession."

For some years consumer groups and legislative bodies have been keenly interested in granting to paramedical personnel—nurses, physicians' assistants, nurse–practitioners—certain rights to render medical care, perform minor surgery, conduct diagnostic examinations, even write prescriptions. The reasoning behind this rather misguided effort is that it will reduce the costs of rendering health care, a matter of some interest especially to those who, as the third party (insurance carrier, government health-care program, prepaid health-maintenance organization), have a vested interest in reducing these costs. Unfortunately, the quality of care declines as well, perhaps proportionately and perhaps disproportionately. The payer isn't too concerned with that; he only deals with the bill. If the care is inferior, you, the patient, are the only one who loses by it. In many cases you may not even get the benefit of the reduced cost because someone else is paying the bill.

However low an opinion you may harbor about the medical profession, the *average* physician has more knowledge and skill than the *average* nurse or physicians' assistant, though it is conceivable that the best one of the latter is better than the worst of the medical profession. But in legal matters, would you be satisfied with the legal secretary or the paralegal assistant, or would you insist on having the *attorney* handle your case?

Another explanation frequently offered for these moves to widen the groups and increase the numbers of people available to render medical care is so that doctors can be spread over greater numbers of patients. I find that reasoning rather fallacious. Carried to an extreme, one could argue that elimination of all doctors except the Surgeon General of the United States would make health care available on a broad scale and at very low cost. But what *kind* of medical care? Would you like to place your health or your life into the hands of a second-year medical student? I was once one of those second-year students, and *I* wouldn't care to.

I expect strenuous objection from the paramedical people to my argument, but I reject their assertion that they know my profession better than, or even as well as, I do. I also don't believe that my patient, having come to me presumably because he or she believes I am a competent doctor, is being fairly treated by being passed on for care to my assistant, subordinate, nurse, or anyone other than me or a physician of equivalent training. Anyone can learn to take a blood pressure measurement, but I have seen it done without any understanding of the procedure at all. The information that results may or may not be accurate or valid. What a pity if it leads to your being given medication you don't really need or which is unsuitable for you, or worse: being given a clean bill of health when, in fact, you should be given treatment.

Anyone can be taught to sew (suture), but there are stitches and there are stitches, in flesh just as in yard goods. There are those who are skillful and those who are not, those who make nearly invisible closures of jagged wounds and those who throw sutures in and leave ugly scars. Some doctors are not so good at suturing, while some physicians' assistants are very good. The odds, however, favor your getting the better job from a doctor—and by a wide margin. If you seek a doctor, you deserve a doctor. If you want a lower fee, you must make the usual choice between "economical" (a doctor with a lower fee) and "cheap" (a person with considerably less training and experience). It's your business, but I feel that you should have the right to make the choice; it should not be made for you, either by legislative bodies or by doctors who, given the right to allow assistants to do their work for them, take advantage of it. I recall a colleague once telling me he "sees" 65–70 patients a day. I told him I do not doubt that 65–70 patients pass through the portals of his office, but I would not for one moment believe that he examines, diagnoses, and treats anything close to that number. Of course, his nurses were "seeing" most of the patients.

There is a small element of risk even in a simple injection, and a certain amount of discomfort associated with the drawing of blood for testing. I cannot tell you how many times I have performed the blood-drawing procedure quickly, easily, and relatively painlessly after my intervention was solicited by a lab technician (or the hapless patient) following countless unsuccessful attempts to find and enter a vein. Am I wonderful? No, but I am a doctor. I have drawn blood thousands of times, many times in the difficult cases when others were unsuccessful. That extra degree of skill is not *always* required. A ten-year-old child with fifteen minutes' training could draw blood from *my* veins, which can be located and entered in total darkness! But some patients are more difficult than others and are fearful of the procedure, and some extra skill is often a blessing.

I used to deal with the screaming terror of children about to get a shot by calmly asking them what they were crying about: they had already had the shot and I was quite finished. They hadn't even felt it in their anguish. Speed, a "light touch," call it what you will, but it is the physician's skill, that which you have a right to expect from *us* but not necessarily from those with one-half or one-quarter the training, any more than you can expect the same degree of surgical skill from the newly graduated doctor as you can from the surgeon who has spent five additional years in surgical training.

CHAPTER 10

A NEW IDEA:
THE RIGHTS OF TEENAGERS

WHEN DID *THEY* GET RIGHTS?

The rights of teenagers? Most of us who are or have been parents of teenagers have been lectured at length about the rights our offspring miraculously acquired on the auspicious occasion of their thirteenth birthdays. We may have questioned our childrens' confusion between rights and privileges. Confirmations and bar/bat mitzvahs, which traditionally take place on or about this time, help to perpetuate the myth that "I Am A Man/Woman." In "Ye Goode Olde Dayes," the rights of minors was a private matter argued, debated, and disputed within the confines of the family unit. But times have changed.

Just as new concepts of informed consent have resulted in taking away the doctor's traditional authoritarian role, so, too, changing values of society have brought forth challenges to the authority of parents. The "Rights of Teenagers" is not a facetious comment but a legal and sociological description of emerging beliefs that have acquired the power and authority of enacted law, whether or not we as individuals agree.

We have long recognized the authority of governments to determine at what age a youngster (called "infant" by the law while still a minor) reaches the age of majority or age of consent. It was automatically assumed that those who had not yet attained this age in their state were incapable of determining what was right or good or best for themselves. It mattered little that the age of consent differed by as much as *seven years* from state to state; that a thirteen-year-old was considered capable of making important decisions in one state, while a twenty-year-old in another state was not.

In recent years, however, sociological, legal, and legislative thinking has changed in several specific areas related to health care. Teens *have* acquired both moral and legal rights that cannot be overruled by parents, teachers, school authorities, or doctors. Despite some rather vigorous resistance on the part of many groups (parents, clergy, and teachers), changing mores of our current society have resulted in not only new concepts but also new laws to enforce them. Doctors find themselves caught in the middle, frequently unaware of the new requirements and resentful of still another challenge to both their own perception of their authority as physicians and their own moral and religious values as parents.

IN WHAT CIRCUMSTANCES DOES THE QUESTION ARISE?

Some situations are easily resolved, for they either pose no great moral dilemma or the problem is really trivial. The first and most obvious one is the matter of emergency care in general. No one seriously questions the right, even the *obligation*, of the physician to render emergency care to a child or adolescent when parental consent is temporarily unavailable. Working parents often cannot be reached instantly, and no doctor could justify, much less legally defend, the sin of omission of critical care on the basis of being unable to obtain proper parental consent in advance. The doctor must, however, be able to show that he tried to contact the parents. All courts recognize his right to act *in loco parentis* (in place of a parent) for the youngster's well-being. Of course this only applies to *emergency* care, not routine care, but the decision as to whether or not an emergency exists is a judgment left to the physician except in most unusual circumstances. Even here, if the matter should be actually carried to the extreme of a lawsuit, the courts are generally lenient in examining the motives of the doctor. If he appears to have acted in the sincere belief that delay would have been harmful to the child, the physician will be exonerated of wrongdoing.

A second concern to doctors, one that ought to be very secondary but often is not, is the matter of payment for the services rendered. Many doctors fear that if a parent is not consulted before treatment, the parent may refuse to pay the bill. In general, it may be assumed that a parent would have acted in the best interest of his or her child and would not, therefore, use the lack of parental consent as a basis for refusing to pay. Likewise, it may be generally but not universally assumed that a parent has an obligation to support a dependent (but not an "independent" or married) child. Nevertheless, some of the laws enacted in the seventies and eighties that grant minors the right to consent to their own treatment and the right to privacy also relieve the parents of financial responsibility in such instances.

Real problems arise, however, in such highly touchy topics as physician–patient contacts where the patient is below the age of majority for a given state and the contact involves matters of sexuality, drug abuse, including alcoholism, or mental problems such as depression. The most common such situations involve a visit by teenagers who desire contraceptive information and a prescription for birth control pills, who are pregnant, or who may have contracted a venereal disease. What now? What is the doctor's position, and what is his or her duty? What responsibilities does the doctor bear, and to whom? Here we enter our brave new world, different from that which we were taught as youngsters or as medical students.

The *legal* situation for the doctor is far from clear or uniform. Different states have recently enacted a variety of laws governing one or more of these situations. Lest you think that minors have been granted extra rights only in those supposedly "backward" states that have long recognized the right to marry without parental consent at such tender ages as fourteen or sixteen, don't. Some of these new laws have been enacted in places we consider sophisticated and conservative.

For example, Massachusetts, long viewed as a center of conservative thought, passed into law in August 1975 House Bill No. 6335, beginning: "AN ACT authorizing the consent by certain minors to certain medical and dental care." Among other things, this law grants to minors the right to give consent without further consultation when "(vi) he reasonably believes himself to be suffering from or to have come in contact with any disease defined as dangerous to the public health . . ." This has been interpreted to include sexually transmitted or venereal disease.

In 1974, Delaware passed House Bill No. 913, which provides that "(a) A minor 12 years of age or over who professes to be afflicted with contagious, infectious, or communicable diseases . . . may give written consent to any licensed physician, hospital, or public clinic for any diagnostic, medical, or surgical care and treatment, including X rays. . . ."

The State of Illinois in 1979 enacted Public Act 81-813,

which states that "a minor 12 years of age or older who may have come into contact with any venereal disease or suffers from the use of depressant or stimulant drugs . . . or narcotic drugs . . . or may be determined to be an alcoholic or an intoxicated person . . . may give consent to the furnishing of medical care or counseling related to the diagnosis or treatment of such disease. . . . The consent of the parent, parents, or legal guardian of such minor shall not be necessary to authorize medical care or counseling."

Virginia's House Bill No. 87 of the Laws of 1978 provides that "(6) *Any person under the age of eighteen years* [emphasis added] may consent to medical or health services required in case of birth control, pregnancy, or family planning, or needed in the care, treatment, or rehabilitation of drug addicts, or other persons who because of the use of controlled drugs are in need of medical care, treatment, or rehabilitation; provided, that the provisions of this subsection shall not apply in the case of vasectomy, salpingectomy ["tying tubes"—Ed.], or other surgical sterilization procedures. . . ."

In general, all states consider as "emancipated," and therefore legally able to consent to their own treatment, adolescents who live apart from their parents, who are financially independent and managing their own resources, who are members of the Armed Forces, who are already married, or who are parents whether married or not. With a display of infinite wisdom, we have concluded that a girl who has already given birth to a child may obtain information about birth control to prevent future pregnancies without having to ask permission of her parents.

PROS AND CONS

But let's look at the dilemma of the doctor whose state laws are not so specific. This doctor is confronted by a fourteen- or fifteen-year-old girl who tells the doctor matter-of-factly that she is sexually active, that she wishes to prevent pregnancy in a reliable manner, and requests a prescription for the Pill. The doctor, of another generation, brought up in a home where religion and school grades, not sex, were the most openly discussed topics, is disturbed, or shocked, or horrified, or repelled. The doctor also knows that birth control pills, containing female sex hormones, are not the best things in the world for an adolescent. What to do?

Let's now speculate that the next visitor is a sixteen-year-old male with painfully obvious evidence of having contracted gonorrhea. The doctor's duty is clear: the young man must be treated, and the law obliges the doctor in most places to report the case to the local or state health authorities. The patient, however, *begs* the doctor not to tell his parents. Later that day, this ill-fated doctor confronts an adolescent female (this hasn't been a great day!). By using a secretly purchased home pregnancy test kit (available in any supermarket, no questions asked), she has just learned the awful truth: she *is*. She asks the doctor to help her get an abortion, and tells him or her she fears for life and limb if her parents find out.

In matters of sexuality, it is most tempting for the doctor to assume the role of surrogate parent, to identify with the parents of the youngster as if the patient were the doctor's own offspring. A doctor can just as easily be convinced to play judge or clergyman and attempt to impose personal moral values on the life-style of the youngster.

Present-day standards impose on the physician the moral duty, and in some states, the legal duty as well, to withhold from the parents any information about their child's medical needs, conditions, or treatments when the child so requests. This is almost a universal requirement when dealing with such topics as sexuality, teenage pregnancy, venereal disease, drug abuse, or alcoholism and their associated psychiatric problems. By doing otherwise the doctor is violating the young patient's right to privacy, now a very definitely recognized "right." From the time of Hippocrates some thirty-five hundred years ago, the physician has been bound to hold in confidence all that he or she learns about a patient in the course of rendering medical care. It is but a small step to carry that duty a millimeter further to cover the teenager, at least where sex, drug, alcohol or psychiatric problems are concerned. Would I be pleased if the patient were my own daughter? Probably not, but thereupon revolves the problem.

One of the questions I advise physicians to ask themselves is whether contacting a parent might result in the child's not returning to receive the necessary treatment or counseling. Teenagers often do not communicate well with adults, and a doctor must consider that if a youngster trusted him or her enough to come in with a troublesome problem, the doctor probably owes the youngster some duty to see that this trust is not violated or abused.

The doctor must also consider whether his own objections are based on some real fact or are merely personal values, which, after all, are supposed to be secondary to medical work. Is the doctor concerned about responsibility and legal liability if untoward effects result from treatment of the child without parental consent or knowledge? Here the laws and precedent court cases of the state must be called upon to clarify the doctor's position. They may enlighten and help, or they may not.

In most states, the physician no longer has any *obligation* to inform parents about a visit by their child, but he or she may ask the youngster for permission to inform the parents. A doctor should use his or her influence as a respected person to show the young patient that the support, concern, and help of the parents would be a good thing, more important than the disapproval and perhaps punishment that might also come about. Sometimes the doctor finds that a young patient welcomes such advice, having feared confronting the parents. The patient may be relieved to have the doctor break the bad news, willing to face the consequences but unwilling or unable to initiate the confrontation. On the other hand, the fears of violence or being put out of the house harbored by some adolescents are very real. Child abuse is a widespread disease among parents, not by any means limited to lower socioeconomic classes. It wouldn't be the first time that the request for birth control pills or for abortion or treatment of venereal disease came about as a result of sexual abuse *within the home*— by the very parent the doctor wants to inform. Adolescents are usually most reluctant to reveal such situations, but can you imagine the consequences to the unfortunate youngster in such a sad situation if the doctor "rats" on her?

On the subject of birth control, we are dealing with a slightly different matter. Here no treatment for an already acquired and existent condition is involved. There is an epidemic of teenage pregnancies (an estimated one million each year), and many nonprescription methods of contraception, some much less effective than prescription methods, are available to anyone in the local drugstore or supermarket drug department. Organizations such as Planned Parenthood will provide information, even prescriptions, without inquiring about the age of their client or violating a confidence. Such organizations believe that neither they nor other doctors will be able to "deactivate" the already sexually active youngster by withholding contraceptive advice and/or products. Grateful that the teen is wise enough to recognize the need for precautions against unwanted pregnancy, they firmly and sincerely believe it is in everyone's best interest to dispense the information and medication or device upon request. If a doctor's moral values prevent him or her, in good conscience, from granting the youngster's request, I believe this doctor's professional duty is to refer the patient elsewhere—to Planned Parenthood, the local public-health clinic, and so on.

"Snitching" to the parent doesn't really help anything, and may hurt a great deal.

We are dealing with several separate and different but related factors. One is the teenagers' rights to request treatment, granted by duly enacted law in many states. Another is the weighing of the effects of denying treatment or withholding contraceptive advice against those of teenage pregnancy, of further dissemination of venereal diseases, or of the potentially tragic results to the youngster, his or her family, and society as a whole, of untreated drug addiction, alcoholism, or depression with its ever-present danger of suicide.

DOCTOR OR PARENT?

Laws grant to teenagers even more freely the right to obtain treatment for nonsexually related problems such as drug abuse, alcoholism, and psychiatric problems. The general feeling is that it is far more important to see that these troubled young people are given care than it is to worry about relatively small matters like informing the parents, even in states where no specific duty to treat on the consent of the minor and/or to hold all information in confidence has yet been imposed by the law. When the doctor ignores the duty of confidentiality despite the requests or pleas of the youngster, is he doing anything more than merely sloughing off onto someone else the responsibility for the youngster and his or her problem? If the doctor tells the parents despite the patient's request for silence, and the doctor's report results in harm to the adolescent, is the doctor free of responsibility?

Admiral Hyman Rickover once remarked:

Responsibility is a unique concept; it can only reside and inhere in a single individual. You may share it with others, but your portion is not diminished. You may delegate it but you cannot divest yourself of it. Even if you do not recognize it or admit its presence, you cannot escape it.

The responsibility here is the responsibility of the doctor to render care to the best of his ability to those who seek it or request it, and to hold in confidence all that he may learn in the course of dealing with his patients. Such declarations are part of the Hippocratic Oath. Our society now recognizes, wisely or otherwise, that teenagers (including, in many instances, persons aged twelve also) do have certain rights distinct and apart from those of their parents. Their right to privacy and confidentiality is recognized, all the more so in matters of sexuality, drug abuse, alcoholism, venereal disease, or mental/nervous distress, which are universally conceded to be highly private matters regardless of who is afflicted and how old he or she may be at the time of affliction.

Finally, I submit that doctors should recognize their special position in such situations. Confidential visits by youngsters may give doctors a unique opportunity for a "one-on-one" discussion with the chance to provide factual information that might otherwise be unavailable to the young person. This may be the youngster's only opportunity to have such a discussion, for too many adolescents are so alienated from their parents and other adults that no such frank exchange is possible. Sometimes it is the *parents* who, for reasons of their own or their upbringing, cannot bring themselves to discuss "hot" topics like sexuality or venereal disease, or who may themselves lack adequate information. The misinformation circulating among teenagers is little short of astonishing.

I once had an opportunity to review a term paper for my son on the subject of contraceptives, an assignment for that classic high school hygiene course in the days when it was not yet called sex ed. After making the necessary revisions to convert it from fantasy to fact, I questioned him about the source of his information, recognizing much of it as the same drivel that circulated among the boys when I was a teenager. I was unprepared for the answer: most of it had come from the school nurse who taught the course and from the brochures she had distributed. I was grateful for the fortuitous opportunity to further my son's education, to help educate his classmates, and apparently to enlighten the school nurse as well.

SO THEY *DO* HAVE RIGHTS!

Having now learned that teenagers have legal rights, how shall we handle this new age of enlightenment? Having demanded all sorts of rights for ourselves as citizens, as consumers, and finally, as patients, can we deny them to others? We recognize that it is wrong to deny rights on the basis of race, religion, national origin, or sex; we are learning that it is also wrong to deny them on the basis of *age*. We can accept that it is unfair and now also illegal to deny individuals their right to work and other rights because they have *passed* some preconceived notion of a mythical upper limit to "useful" life. The moralists and the legislatures now also tell us that we must use similar reasoning in the opposite direction: we must grant certain rights to those who have not yet attained an equally mystical (and quite variable) minimum age of intelligence, enlightenment, or what-have-you. Is it right or wrong? Time will judge that. For the moment, it is probably not a question of either, but rather of the relative benefits, or conversely, of the relative risks, of "allowing" youngsters these rights already granted by law in many places, as contrasted with turning away, playing ostrich, and saying, as I have heard many parents declare: "If you don't teach them about birth control and don't make contraceptives available, they won't engage in sex." Good luck. It brings to mind an incident some years back when the local Girl Scout troop scheduled a showing of a GSA film on menstruation with commentary and a question-and-answer session afterward to be conducted by me. It was canceled at the last minute because of objections of some parents who did not think their tender-aged daughters should be told about "The Curse." I couldn't help but wonder if they truly believed that girls who are not told about menstruation wouldn't menstruate.

The right to know has, it seems, become another of our "inalienable rights" along with the right to privacy, though Thomas Jefferson may never have envisioned such extensions of his awe-inspiring words in the Declaration of Independence. I am not sure *where* and *how* our youngsters began to acquire these rights, but they most assuredly have them now, for better or for worse. I think for better when all is said and done. They often have the erroneous impression that they have acquired *exclusive* rights denied to us, the adults. Not so.

Before leaving this topic, however, I would be remiss in *my* duty of full disclosure if I did not discuss a small detail highly relevant to the matter of the rights of young people that is "floating about" at the time I write this.

The Reagan Administration has made known a proposal to establish a federal regulation that would *require* any federally funded or federally assisted clinic giving out information about birth control to minors to inform the parents of the youngster. The news was greeted with an uproar by a wide variety of groups, hailed by some religious leaders, denounced by other people, some organized, some individual voices.

Planned Parenthood promptly responded by announcing that if such a regulation were put into effect, they would renounce all federal funding rather than accede. They stated emphatically that they felt it was their avowed responsibility to give information about birth control to any and all who requested it, and always in the strictest of confidence. They felt most strongly that the problem of teenage pregnancy was the real culprit, and any thoughts about telling parents or denying the information on the basis of age rather than need (i.e., sexual activity) was very wrong.

The American College of Obstetricians and Gynecologists (ACOG) proclaimed that the plan "makes no sense on the grounds of health," explaining that teenage females face a five times greater chance of serious illness and death as a result of pregnancy than from birth control pills or IUDs. Testifying on behalf of eight organizations, the ACOG president said many teenagers would not seek birth control services if they knew their parents would be notified. Furthermore, he added, such a regulation would tend to discriminate against the poor, for youngsters from more affluent families could obtain the advice from private physicians, whereas the public clinics might be the only resource available to the poor.

Whether this regulation will ever be put into effect cannot be known at this time, but it has generated strong opposition and controversy. At the very least, it will be a long time coming. The regulation does seem to be a step back into the past, and given the realities of the alternatives, it does not appear to be a realistic approach to reestablishing "lost" moral values.

CHAPTER 11

FEDERAL REGULATION

Drugs—their manufacture, prescription, and use—are sometimes a part of malpractice suits, and federal regulation helps decide what drug is prescribed for your illness. No agency of the federal government has any direct statutory authority to regulate the practice of medicine. Such power is reserved to the individual states through professional licensing bodies, but the federal government plays a major role in regulating drugs.

THE FOOD AND DRUG ADMINISTRATION (FDA)

The Food and Drug Administration (FDA) operates by authority of the Food, Drug and Cosmetic Act of 1938, amended in 1962 and again in 1976. This law grants to the FDA, a division of what is now the Department of Health and Human Services, the power to supervise and regulate the manufacture, distribution, promotion, and claims for medications and health products, diagnostic products, and medical instruments and devices; the power to regulate the manufacture and claims but not the advertising (reserved to the Federal Trade Commission) of nonprescription medications; and the power to regulate, but to a much lesser degree (restricted primarily to safety matters), the production of food additives and cosmetics. The mandate of the 1938 law was for the FDA to ensure the *safety*, in a rather perfunctory manner, of prescription medications before permitting them to enter general use. After the thalidomide tragedy of the early 1960s, Congress amended the act. As a result, much more stringent standards were required to substantiate the utility of any new drug: manufacturers were required to prove and document *efficacy* as well as safety of all prescription and nonprescription drugs, old and new; and to strengthen the FDA's authority to ensure compliance. A number of court cases, including several that reached the Supreme Court of the United States, determined conclusively that the FDA is the final authority for decisions that must be based on *scientific* evidence. The 1976 amendments further expanded the authority of the FDA to cover medical instruments and devices.

Federal regulations promulgated to implement the acts of Congress have spelled out in ever-increasing complexity the manner in which new drugs and devices must be tested before an application for marketing can be approved, the extent to which the manufacturer or distributor may make advertising claims for the product, the necessity of FDA approval of the wording of the official "labeling"—which includes both the package label and the "package insert" that must be included in every package of a prescription drug—the manner in which such products may be manufactured, and the actions the FDA may take when information is received through field inspections or other sources that reveals serious violations that might endanger the user of the product. Also new were the requirements for continued follow-up and annual reporting to detect adverse experiences or side effects that might become evident after approval.

A broad review of *all* medications on the market in 1962 was undertaken. For prescription drugs, this was conducted jointly by the National Academy of Sciences and the National Research Council under the name Drug Efficacy Study Implementation. Following the recommendations of these groups, the FDA has classified all such drugs as "Effective"; "Probably Effective" (but requiring some additional research to fully document its effectiveness); "Possibly Effective" (serious doubts exist, but the manufacturer is given the opportunity to produce supportive evidence that the drug does work as claimed); and "Ineffective" (must be immediately withdrawn from general use). Though almost two decades have elapsed since this program began, implementation has not yet been completed. This is due, in part, to continuing research to prove effectiveness, and to the initiation of many lawsuits against the FDA by the manufacturers. Such lawsuits further delay final implementation of FDA action. In most instances, the government eventually prevails, but the time consumed in bringing the case to trial, filing appeals, and so on, permits continued marketing of the allegedly "possibly effective" drugs.

In early 1982, the FDA finally began the lengthy and involved regulatory process that should result in the withdrawal from the market of all medications originally evaluated and categorized as "probably Effective" or "Possibly Effective." Though many such evaluations were not completed for nearly a decade after the law was revised in 1962, twenty years have now passed since the legal requirements were enacted, and it is high time some of these allegedly ineffective drugs were removed from circulation. If there was evidence that they worked, it should have been clearly established by now.

A few years back, the FDA established additional review panels made up of government, consumer, and industry representatives and medical experts to review all nonprescription (over-the-counter, or OTC) health products— the ones you can buy off the supermarket shelves. This work is still in progress. Eventually, it is hoped that all medications and medical devices available to the patient, either via a doctor's prescription or order, or by direct purchase from pharmacy or supermarket, will have been reviewed and found acceptable, and will have been shown to be safe and effective within the context of their intended use.

Much criticism has been voiced against the FDA by consumer groups and congressional committees on the one hand for failure to act quickly enough, and by pharmaceutical manufacturers on the other for acting too hastily, or for acting at all! The FDA procedures do seem to take considerable, perhaps even unreasonable, time to implement, but the time required is probably no more, relative to the enormous complexity of the task, than any other process that must snail-crawl its way through the maze of government bureaucracy. Still, while regulation undoubtedly results in the public interest, overregulation may slip in with the greatest of ease, increasing costs without providing an equivalent increase in consumer protection. In fact, too much regulation can and does result in manufacturers finding ways to evade it altogether, making the regulatory process counterproductive and leading to no regulation at all.

Consumer criticism is also heard about the time required for a new drug application to be approved and the drug released for general use. Often these drugs have been in widespread use in Europe and elsewhere for years, and the public wonders why we in the United States are denied the "benefits" of new treatments. The inevitable reply of the FDA is that thalidomide, too, was in use in Europe and elsewhere for some years before its potential for harm was noticed, and while this argument is becoming tiresome, it nonetheless carries a degree of common sense with it. To be sure, the FDA is overly cautious, but not without good reason, and the eventual good probably outweighs much of the inconvenience caused by the delays.

Federal regulations require that the FDA render a decision on an application for approval of a new drug within 180 days from its receipt at its headquarters in a Washington, D.C., suburb. Though this time period is not infrequently extended because of questions about the data, or because the FDA scientists and reviewing officers feel some additional data are necessary before they can make a realistic decision that is fair to both sides, much if not most of the delay time in bringing a new drug to the market is consumed by prolonged periods of testing. At times, this seems to be far more than efficient research management should require. Currently, it is estimated that the average "new drug" requires five to seven years and over $15 million of research from the time it emerges from the early animal testing laboratories until the application is filed.

While the FDA has the power to regulate which drugs are released for general use, and the power to specify what claims may be made, it has *no power* to dictate the manner in which any approved drug is used by a practicing physician. If a doctor's knowledge or experience suggests that the drug may be useful in conditions other than the "approved" ones, or that doses in excess of the maximum "recommended" ones may be helpful in certain situations, the physician is legally free to render such judgments and practice medicine accordingly—so long as nothing goes wrong!

While not "legally binding" in court, the documented allegation that your doctor prescribed or administered a drug in excess of the manufacturer's FDA-approved recommendations, or in a manner or for an indication other than those "approved," and that you suffered injury resulting from that nonconforming use of the medication is mighty convincing to a judge or jury as evidence of malpractice. As in other instances cited, the doctor's judgment becomes a much weaker argument than documentation from manufacturer's labeling, medical texts, and more than likely, the testimony of medical experts that such use of the medication is *not* consistent with the usual standards of medical practice. If you were a member of the jury, how would you vote? I am a physician deeply involved in new drug research and compliance with government regulations. While I would sympathize (empathize?) with the doctor's obviously good intentions, I would probably have to conclude that he took on the risk, and if it resulted in injury to the patient, is liable for compensation.

You should be aware that if your doctor had presented you in advance with the clear knowledge that the medication, higher dosage, or new use was experimental or investigational, that its eventual safety and effectiveness had not been determined as yet, and you granted informed consent to "try it," the doctor has little if any liability so long as the medicine was administered in the manner prescribed by the research protocol—the *recipe* if you will —that was provided by the manufacturer for carrying out the research project. In the first instance, the use was at the doctor's own risk, whereas in the second illustration, it was clearly a trial use to which you agreed and consented. Should you wonder why in the world any fool would volunteer for such experimentation, muse for a moment on this hypothetical (but often seen in real life) situation: a patient confronted by a diagnosis of cancer that has been deemed incurable by known and proven methods is offered the opportunity to participate in the trials of a new anti-cancer agent whose safety and effectiveness are not yet fully known, but which *might* help the patient to survive. Would you accept under *these* conditions? There are, of course, many other less dramatic scenarios in which a patient could justifiably agree to participate in the clinical trials of a new drug or new use of an "old" drug without appearing to have taken leave of his senses. It's a good thing, too, for otherwise we would have no means of testing such new medications or new uses except in laboratory animals, and these results are not always the same as in humans.

Malpractice suits against doctors not infrequently allege negligence for the occurrence of serious side effects from the use of a drug about which the patient had not been warned. Sometimes such suits are justified, but just as often, they describe adverse experiences that were not generally recognized as associated with the medication at the time it was prescribed. The determining factor as to whether or not malpractice occurred may be whether or not the side effect was included in the manufacturer's labeling. Such suits are more commonly, and more properly, directed against the manufacturer of the drug for "having failed to adequately test it, or having done so, for having failed to advise the medical profession of the potential danger." Circumstances vary greatly, and some of these cases are won by the plaintiffs. Others are not. Among the more notorious drug-related cases were those implicating the antibiotic chloramphenicol as the cause of irreversibly fatal aplastic anemia (destruction of the red-blood-corpuscle-forming organs). The antibiotic had been in widespread use and was at one time commonly prescribed for many simple upper-respiratory infections. It is still on the market, but its use is wisely restricted to certain severe illnesses where it remains the best drug available, and where the risk of the treatment is far less than the risk of the disease treated by less effective means.

THE DRUG PACKAGE INSERT

Does the "package insert," the official labeling of a medication, have in and of itself any legal force? When applied to the licensed physician, the answer is no. In the context of a malpractice suit, as we have noted earlier, it may be introduced as evidence, but must take its place on the scales of justice along with all other evidence and expert testimony. Any special importance attributed to it lies in the belief of the judge or jury that it has special significance to the incident worthy of consideration in arriving at a final decision or verdict.

A few cases have been tried in which the plaintiff's arguments have relied heavily on the recommendations of the official labeling, but in each case, other extenuating circumstances were present such that it was not possible to determine how large a part the labeling played in reaching the verdict. No doubt we shall see other such cases brought to trial in the years to come, and a clearer doctrine of "precedent-case" law will emerge.

For now, the official labeling represents only the manufacturer's recommendations based on research, and the government's ruling on the drug's usefulness and safety. Even "safe" is subject to varying interpretations. We will tolerate side effects in a life-saving drug (for example, chemotherapy for cancer) that would be totally unacceptable in a drug whose principal use is to assist in weight-reduction programs or the relief of cold symptoms.

For a verdict of malpractice, it is necessary to show not just that a doctor has used a medication in a manner other than that recommended by the manufacturer, but that doing so caused the patient some injury that was entirely a result of the drug use and not contributed to by the patient's illness, actions, or failure to follow advice.

GENERIC DRUGS

Mandatory substitution laws now exist in many states whereby the pharmacist is *obliged* to fill your brand-name prescription with a less expensive generic drug unless the prescribing physician has specifically prohibited the generic drug by written and signed order.

The confusion and conflicting arguments in the public mind is matched by an equally furious controversy in the scientific world about the *equivalence* of generic drugs. Just what *is* a generic drug? It is the chemical compound or combination of chemical compounds that constitute a certain medication, sold under its recognized chemical name rather than the brand name of a specific manufacturer. It is a "house brand" or a "Brand X." Liken it to a household appliance manufactured by a major or minor manufacturer of such appliances, but sold under the private brand of a large department store or discount store chain, or the private-label canned foods sold by some large supermarket chains. They are not necessarily identical to the brand-name ones. The chain may have specified some cost-cutting measures in order to sell the appliances or other goods at a lower price. Are they "as good as" the branded variety? Eventually the purchaser must make that decision. They might even be better!

Is a generic drug the *same* as a branded variety? It may be, or it may not. The *active* ingredients are the same—the label says so—but these are not the only ingredients in the product. To produce a tablet, a capsule, a liquid preparation, or an ointment, certain other substances, called excipients, are used to come up with the desired finished product. These excipients are not entirely without function, and may affect the speed with which a tablet dissolves, the rate at which the active ingredient(s) is absorbed into the bloodstream, and even the rate at which the medication is destroyed by or excreted from the body. Since the speed with which they become available in the bloodstream and the length of time they remain in the body intact are critical to the manner in which they can do their intended job, drugs that are identical in name, that contain the same active ingredients but different excipients or are manufactured by different processes, may *not* be biologically or therapeutically equivalent at all.

How can you know? There is no good general answer to this question as yet. Many factors come into play, and as a rule, the patient is in no position to know or evaluate any of them. Sometimes the pharmacist can make such an evaluation, and sometimes he or she has ulterior motives. Sometimes the FDA knows the pros and cons, but it, too, can have ulterior motives, since the government pays for the medical care of a large segment of the population and in the near future might be paying for the medical care of nearly everyone. Even doctors have no way of knowing the difference between brand-name drugs and generics other than what they hear or read, and that information may have been quite prejudiced one way or the other, depending on its source.

It is a fact that *some* generic drugs come out of the very same production machinery as the brand-name product, being produced by the large pharmaceutical company in "private label" containers for distribution by others as generic drugs. Can you find this out? Not easily, for the labeling requirements of the Food, Drug and Cosmetic Act and federal regulations stipulate that the name of the manufacturer *or* the distributor must be clearly shown, but not both. "Manufactured for . . ." is the usual legend on the label. This may be changed in the near future by proposed new federal regulations.

Some generic drugs are manufactured by companies

that specialize in producing high-quality medications for private-label distribution only. In all likelihood, their products are every bit as good as the brand names, but since these firms manufacture only drugs that have been around for some time and are no longer under patent protection, and they make no expenditures for research to develop new compounds, their costs of operations, which eventually are supposed to determine the price of the drug, are much lower than those of the large, research-oriented pharmaceutical firms. The price of their drugs is always lower, but their profit margin might be much *higher*.

In common with most large industries, the pharmaceutical companies are often accused of inflating the selling price of their drugs because of the "operating expenses" of high-living executives, enormous outlays for advertising, the support of product-slanted educational programs for doctors, and other such excesses. But I have been personally responsible for organizing hundreds of such educational programs paid for by pharmaceutical firms and have never produced one that was more promotional than generally educational. Often, the pharmaceutical firms are the principal, or even the *only*, source of funds for postgraduate medical education at the grass-roots level.

If there is any one area where large outlays of money tend to inflate the selling price of drugs, it is in the area of expenditure for research. Not every drug for which millions of dollars are laid out ends up as a viable product. Some are abandoned when the clinical trials reveal dangers that had not been apparent earlier. There is no source of funds for these research costs except the revenues from the sale of products that *do* reach the market. Another factor in drug prices is that pharmaceutical manufacturing, whether for branded or generic distribution, has traditionally been highly profitable. The large manufacturers blame much of the high cost of drugs on the high costs of complying with government regulations, and that is undoubtedly partly true.

But how significant *is* the difference in price between a branded drug and its generic partner (I have carefully avoided the use of the word *equivalent*)? A wholesale drug firm that sells only to licensed physicians and hospitals listed in a recent catalogue the following prices for a popular tranquilizer whose patent has run out: brand name, $11.70 per 100; generic, $1.50 per 100. Are they equivalent? I don't know. If a series of patient trials demonstrates that the generic medication has as good an effect as the branded version, I would be convinced. The decision on whether or not to buy a generic drug must rest with you, the patient. Unfortunately, you have no sound basis on which to make it and could only agree with me that for an investment of $1.50, the generic drug may be worth a try. But then again, you might want to be sure of getting the expected relief from the medication and might *not* wish to "give it a try."

There is a time when such factors might play a role in a malpractice suit. Instances have been uncovered where a pharmacy dispenses a less costly generic drug but charges for the branded variety, and even instances when a pharmacy has typed the *brand name* on the vial! If your treatment failure (your failure to obtain relief of symptoms or resolution of an illness) can be demonstrated beyond a reasonable doubt to be the result of such an unauthorized and concealed substitution, you could have excellent grounds for a lawsuit—against the pharmacist.

The law is far less likely to prevail in your favor if the generic substitution was made with the doctor's knowledge and permission, and you have little or no chance of success with a lawsuit if the substitution was made under a state law *requiring* such substitutions. The argument that your doctor *could have* overruled the law and prohibited substitutions will hold little weight in court, especially if the substituted generic appears on some state or federal list of authorized and acceptable substitutions. This is a most flagrant example of government "interference" with the practice of medicine, and even the practice of pharmacy, but it has, for the moment at least, the authority of the law. Intensive scientific testing would be necessary to demonstrate to the court's satisfaction that the generic substitute was inadequate. Such testing would cost far more than your lawsuit budget could consider reasonable, and it might serve no useful purpose when completed.

What should you do about generic substitution or generic preference? Ask a lot of questions—of your doctor and your pharmacist. Try to detect how much confidence each of them has in the generic, then decide how much the "risk" is worth to you in terms of the money you are willing to pay for your prescription. What do I do? I use and prescribe generics—sometimes. And sometimes I insist on the branded drug because I have come to respect its quality and dependability and to doubt the reliability of those particular generic substitutes. But remember that because of the unusual nature of my work, I have a great deal more information about generic "equivalence" than is available to most doctors in practice.

Statistics, which are well known to have the ability to bend this way or that to "prove" the desires of the interpreter of the data, claim that the number of "recalls" ordered by the FDA in recent years is far greater for drugs manufactured by generic houses than it is for those from research-oriented firms. A recall occurs when the FDA orders the manufacturer to remove or recall from distributors and pharmacies all containers of a certain drug or a certain production lot of a given drug because of some defect or violation of law. The defect might be an incorrect label, perhaps relatively inconsequential (though illegal nevertheless), or it might represent a real hazard to health or even to life, such as when the label lists a much lower or higher strength tablet than the ones contained in the bottle. There are even occasional really serious problems when the bottle contains a medication *other than* the one specified on the label. The defect might be insolubility of the tablets because they were too heavily compressed in the manufacturing process or some other less accidental reason. I have known of cases where plaster of Paris was used as an excipient instead of a more suitable, and more costly, ingredient. The tablets could be recovered, still intact, from the stools.

For so long as the controversy among scientists continues on this subject, I cannot resolve it with a few simple words. Be assured, in any event, that with hindsight we shall one day be able to see clearly the overall value, balancing price against effectiveness, of generic substitutions. In the meantime, be suspicious of whatever you read or hear on the subject, and do not be taken in by those who have vested interests in opposing generic substitution or those who think generics are the one and only way to go.

CHAPTER 12

AUTHORITY OVER PHYSICIANS

THE AMA

One of the most widely held misconceptions about the medical profession is the supposed authority of the American Medical Association to govern and control the practices, philosophies, beliefs, and behavior of physicians. Such comments as "the strongest union in the country"; "keeps the number of physicians down so each one can earn more money"; and "some doctors would like to change the system but the AMA won't let them" are commonly heard in every part of the nation. Is there much truth to them? Is there *any* truth to them? Here are some facts that may startle you.

The American Medical Association is a professional organization, privately owned by its members, which acts as a policy-*suggesting* body for the medical profession. It has no legal authority whatsoever over the conduct of its members. It speaks as "The Voice of Medicine," yet numbers barely half of the physicians in the United States among its membership. Physicians are under no obligation to belong to it, and vast numbers of them choose not to be associated with it or its statements of policy. It does not control the number of students admitted to medical school, the number of medical schools in the country, or the criteria for admission practiced by any of them. It has no voice in granting licenses to practice or in controlling the number of such licenses granted. It has no authority to insist that its members subscribe to or follow the policies and philosophies it advocates. It has no authority to "strike" or to request or order that its membership or any portion of it go on strike. It cannot engage in collective bargaining in any sense of the term on behalf of its members, and certainly not for the medical profession as a whole. In essence, its power is minimal, its influence declining, and its authority almost nonexistent.

What is it, then? Why do we hear so much about it? Principally, it is a vocal lobbying organization that, like all such private-interest groups, attempts to influence legislators (in a perfectly legal manner inherent in our democratic way of life) to its way of thinking. Why do we hear it mentioned so often? It speaks *loudly,* if not always well.

Are there any good things to say about it? *Absolutely!* It publishes some of the finest medical journals in the world. It maintains one of the best informed law departments to advise both doctors and lawyers on medical–legal matters. It assists in setting the standards for specialty board certification by which doctors are granted the right to identify themselves as specialists in a specific field of medicine. It assists its members and the medical profession at large in any professional matters for which a doctor might desire and seek its guidance. It suggests ethical standards of practice, but has no authority to enforce them. It endorses the administration of two physicians' "oaths," but they were written by Hippocrates of Greece (fifth to fourth century B.C.) and Rabbi Moses ben Maimon of Spain, also known as Maimonides the Physician (about A.D. 1200). And for those doctors who subscribe to its policies regarding such controversial subjects as national health insurance, it speaks with a mighty voice, though only by the slimmest margin may it be said to speak for the "majority" of American doctors.

If you suspect a doctor has been guilty of ethical misconduct, you cannot complain to the AMA, for it can do nothing. If you sue a doctor unreasonably, the doctor cannot complain to the AMA, for it can do nothing.

Is it expensive to belong? Rather so. Is it worth it? Only for the doctor who believes that the AMA speaks for *him* or *her*, for the doctor who agrees with what the AMA Congress of Delegates decides should be its "policy" on any matter.

It publishes an evaluation of medications commonly prescribed in this country. The volume has a certain degree of authority even in the courtroom, but not necessarily because it is published by the AMA. Its credibility comes mainly from the panel of outstanding experts that has been assembled to write the book and update it from time to time. In some instances, the book disagrees with other respected reference books. In a few instances, it may even disagree with official FDA-approved labeling for some drugs. It may be submitted as evidence in a trial, but bears no more weight than any other recognized treatise on medicine, expert testimony, or other acceptable forms of evidence.

On purely medical, nonpolitical matters, the AMA provides a forum for serious scientific discussion and at times disagreement. If it did nothing else, this alone would suffice to justify its existence, for many topics in medicine are neither black nor white, but are subject to varying opinions. A central, recognized, and respected forum to discuss conflicting research results and impressions is necessary if we are to arrive at that which is most likely to be closest to "best," most of the time, for most of the patients, at our present level of knowledge.

The American Medical Association has a long and not always enviable record of being behind the times, of continuing to voice opposition to programs of social welfare whose time had come, for better or for worse. It opposed the Social Security system when it was first proposed by Franklin Delano Roosevelt during the early thirties. It opposed the Medicare and Medicaid programs in John F. Kennedy's term. It opposes national health insurance as it is usually conceived by the population and proposed by the politicians in our own time. Of course, the AMA was hardly the only group to oppose these measures, and there are many even today who find great faults in one or all of these programs, which were used as examples only because they are familiar to everyone. It cannot even be said—yet—that the AMA was wrong each time, if there can even be a "right" or a "wrong" stand on such issues, for the recipients of the benefits and the payers of the costs have quite conflicting interests.

Whatever your opinion of the American Medical Association, it is *not* the doctor's "union" or the controlling organization in American medicine.

STATE AND COUNTY MEDICAL SOCIETIES

These professional organizations, while "affiliated" with the American Medical Association, are autonomous groups that are far more representative of America's doctors. Because the county medical association is the principal policing agency of doctors' ethical practices, membership is required for appointment to most hospital staffs, and membership in the county medical society usually carries automatic membership in the state medical society.

It is the county medical society that maintains committees to hear patient grievances of *any* nature, including those regarding the size of fees, which may be lodged against a physician. All such grievances are given careful consideration, and the doctor is called to explain his or her actions or justify the fee. The committee's "verdict" carries no legal authority with it, but it does exert sufficient pressure on the doctor usually to result in acceptance of the decision. After all, when a doctor's own county medical society feels the patient is justified in making a complaint, it is difficult for the doctor to remain stubborn. These grievance committees, by the way, may also hear complaints lodged by one doctor against another, of which there may be a steady flow in the course of a year. This is really the only place such grievances can be heard and resolved. They include such complaints as: "patient stealing"—deliberate efforts by one doctor to cast innuendoes or untrue aspersions on the competence or character of another doctor, inducing the latter's patient to leave his or her care; discrimination without just cause in hospital staff appointments or promotions when the situation cannot be solved within the hospital itself; and other such matters in the general run of angers and frustrations of one mortal toward another that inevitably occur in the course of close professional dealings.

It is the county medical society that maintains a malpractice review committee and that provides the panel physicians for pretrial hearings and reviews where such hearings are the custom or are mandated by state law or court rules.

The societies also provide a forum for dissemination of information and discussion of all matters of interest to physicians, including personal insurance coverage at group rates, new scientific knowledge, and updating on political or legislative matters.

The state medical society is simply a larger body composed of representatives from the affiliated county societies with the obviously greater resources for carrying out the activities described in the preceding paragraphs. A state society's annual scientific assembly can attract lecturers and exhibitors that would not be available to the much smaller county groups. The state society also has better contact with state legislators to make known the opinions and desires of the state's doctors, and conversely, to report back to the membership on legislative proceedings that might affect medical practice.

Both county and state medical societies are far more "grass roots" in character and are therefore more representative of the medical profession than the AMA. They also include close to 100 percent of licensed physicians in their membership rosters, in marked contrast to AMA membership.

Upon a finding of a serious breach of ethics or law on the part of a physician, county or state societies may bring the matter to the attention of the state licensing authorities for further investigation and possible legal action. County and state societies are extremely sensitive to the conduct of their members and are among the most severely self-policing professional organizations found anywhere, though this self-policing is not always as effective as it should be and as we would wish it to be.

The county societies in particular are a wise place for initial discussion about a serious grievance against a doctor when it is still questionable whether malpractice may have been committed. Many patients hesitate to approach such societies, fearing the "conspiracy of silence," but they are surprised at the cooperative effort made on their behalf. In fact, county societies often respond with stronger disciplinary action to complaints lodged by patients than they do to complaints from lawyers or other doctors. This is in part due to a degree of appreciation that the patient, initially at least, has selected this route rather than the direct road to the courtroom. Doctors are not against patients so much as they are against *litigation,* and they are far more willing to see the wronged patient receive his or her just due without recourse to the legal process.

STATE LICENSING BOARDS

They call themselves by different names and are divisions of a great variety of governmental agencies in the different states, but they represent the *sole legal authority* governing the practice of medicine and the ethical conduct of physicians. In New York, they are the Bureau of Professional Licensing, a division of the State Department of Education. In New Jersey, they pertain to the Department of Law and Safety, Division of Consumer Affairs. But regardless of the name, the function is the same: to determine by suitable means who has demonstrated the necessary formal education, training, and qualifications and is of proper moral character to be granted the privilege of practicing medicine and to identify those who violate the trust placed in them and are no longer worthy of the privilege.

Our American sense of individual liberties has from time to time resulted in challenges to the constitutionality of all professional licensing. Opponents have argued that refusing a license to anyone constitutes a violation of the Fourteenth Amendment. The definitive pronouncement on the subject, however, was made by the Supreme Court of the United States in the case of Dent *v.* West Virginia, heard in 1889. It may be of interest to read the Court's decision, reproduced here verbatim. The Court, speaking through Justice Field, declared:

> It is undoubtedly the right of every citizen of the United States to follow any lawful calling, business, or profession he may choose, subject only to such restrictions as are imposed upon all persons of like age, sex and condition. This right may in many respects be considered as a distinguishing feature of our republican institutions. Here all vocations are open to every one on like conditions. All

may be pursued as sources of livelihood, some requiring years of study and great learning for their successful prosecution. The interests, or as it is sometimes termed, the estate acquired in them, that is, the right to continue their prosecution, is often of great value to possessors, and cannot be arbitrarily taken from them, any more than their real or personal property can be thus taken. But there is no arbitrary deprivation of such right where its exercise is not permitted because of a failure to comply with conditions imposed by the State for protection of society. The power of the State to provide for the general welfare of its people authorizes it to prescribe all such regulations, as in its judgement, will secure or tend to secure them against the consequences of ignorance and incapacity as well as of deception and fraud. As one means to this end it has been the practice of different states from time immemorial, to exact in many pursuits a certain degree of skill and learning upon which the community may confidently rely, their possession being generally ascertained upon an examination of parties by competent persons, or inferred from a certificate to them in the form of a diploma or license from an institution established for instruction on the subjects, scientific and otherwise, with which such pursuits have to deal. The nature and extent of the qualifications required must depend primarily upon the judgement of the State as to their necessity. If they are appropriate to the call or profession, and attainable by reasonable study or application, no objection to their validity can be raised because of their stringency or difficulty. It is only when they have no relation to such calling or profession, or are unattainable by such reasonable study and application, that they can operate to deprive one of his right to pursue a lawful vocation.[1]

The purpose of licensing of doctors is to prevent incompetent, insufficiently educated, or unscrupulous persons from practicing the profession. But it is a privilege granted

[1] 129 U.S. 114, 121–122, 9 S. Ct. 231 (1889).

by the state upon satisfactory demonstration of qualifications and character, and as such the license is subject to suspension or revocation by the individual state for good cause. The *grounds* for revocation are spelled out in the various state licensing acts and include such things as conviction of a felony, unprofessional conduct, and mental or physical incapacity. The first named is a finite statement of fact and leaves no room for discussion or dispute. The last named must be subject to the most careful and profound scrutiny by persons knowledgeable about such evaluations, which, in this instance, can only be physicians.

Unprofessional conduct, on the other hand, is a most vague and indefinite term. The different state licensing acts attempt to define it for the guidance of their licensing agencies in applying the term, but it remains most subjective, and subject to a great variety of interpretations. Among the areas often included in this category are gross malpractice (implying very severe acts, habitual acts, or acts indicative of gross incompetence in general; certainly not every single act of malpractice is grounds for revocation of license); deceptive claims and promises (intended to deal with the charlatan who acts like the medicine man of old); advertising or soliciting patients, though recently published regulations of the Federal Trade Commission appear to be heralding a new era of thought on this subject; and "improper association with others in obtaining or handling business," a subtitle that addresses such matters as contracting with ambulance drivers for referrals, fee-splitting, and so on. With doctors as busy as they are these days, acts of solicitation are rarely the subject of license suspension investigations anymore. On the other hand, the increased freedom of our present-day society has brought forth a new cause of such proceedings rarely seen in the past: sexual advances toward the patient, which are an abuse of the special situation in which the medical practitioner often finds himself, in the presence of a disrobed patient. Incidentally, this is also a violation of one of the tenets of the Hippocratic Oath; perhaps it was a problem even then.

As indefinite as the descriptions are of "unprofessional conduct," a doctor cannot be deprived of his or her license capriciously or without due process of law. A careful investigation of the facts and allegations must be conducted, a formal hearing must be held, and the doctor must be allowed the opportunity to present a defense in his or her own behalf—a person is innocent, of course, until proven guilty. A doctor who disagrees with the decision of the licensing agency has recourse to the courts for a review of the matter.

Does license revocation happen often? Not very often, but the offenses required are serious and are not *committed* very often. Do doctors tend to protect each other? Probably. Humans tend to relate to their colleagues and to "cover up for their buddies." Who among us has never told a supervisor that the fellow at the next desk, table, or machine "just stepped out" when in fact he was taking an extended lunch hour, or told a friend's spouse that there was a bad traffic jam on the way home when the friend had really stopped for a drink? We even have a name for such actions—white lies—and we are taught as young children that certain extenuating circumstances condone untruths or half-truths for the purpose of protecting companions or the feelings of others. This is not exactly a conspiracy of silence!

It is a most difficult decision for doctors to take the first step that may lead to revocation of the license of a colleague, especially when the grounds are incapacity or impairment. Somehow we can accept misconduct better, probably because we feel it is willful, whereas incapacity is involuntary and rarely recognized by the person afflicted with it. An old joke went that if you thought you were crazy, you probably weren't, because if you really were, you wouldn't be capable of recognizing that you were.

I mentioned in passing in an earlier chapter that the patient who hauls a truly incompetent or incapacitated doctor into court may be doing the doctor, the doctor's colleagues, and the doctor's patients a service. It is an unfortunate and brutal means of reaching a justified end, but sometimes the colleagues heave a great sigh of relief that the burden of exposing their friend has been lifted from *them*. To have been exposed by a patient, by the victim of the incompetence or incapacity, somehow seems more just than to be "snitched on" by a fellow doctor. Before any of us became physicians, every one of us was a person, subject to all the frailties and weaknesses of all mortals, Deity Complex or no Deity Complex.

CHAPTER 13

SOME FINAL THOUGHTS

The right of every citizen to seek compensation for wrongful acts or acts of negligence committed on him or her is fundamental to our American way of life. But when dissatisfaction is not the result of negligence, there is no inherent right to compensation, no matter how well off the doctor may be or how good an insurance policy the doctor may have.

Malpractice cases, in common with other types of personal-injury lawsuits, have grown out of all proportion to reality, as is well recognized by leaders of both the legal and the medical professions. Medical malpractice lawsuits are rarely seen in other countries, whose doctors look at us and wonder what the devil is going on over here.

Warren Burger, Chief Justice of the Supreme Court of the United States, expressed concern for this deplorable state of affairs in 1976. He warned that "new ways must be found to provide reasonable compensation for injuries resulting from negligence of hospitals and doctors, without the distortion in the cost of medical and hospital care witnessed in the past few years. . . . New ways must be found to compensate people for injuries from negligence of others without having the process take years to complete and consume up to half of the damages awarded."[1]

But repeated efforts of researchers to define the cause or causes of the problem conclude that the crisis is probably *not* due primarily to ungrateful patients, greedy lawyers, unsympathetic judges, or juries that do not understand the facts. Both plaintiffs' and defense attorneys agree that juries tend to understand medical matters reasonably well —much better than they understand the *legal* issues involved. Plaintiffs' attorneys hold a widespread belief that juries are prejudiced in favor of the doctor–defendant, while defense attorneys insist that juries are prejudiced *against* doctors.

Each of the factors mentioned above is undoubtedly responsible for specific malpractice lawsuits, verdicts, and awards, but these factors are not the major causes of the great proliferation of malpractice litigation. Careful investigators in both the medical and the legal professions conclude time and time again that most malpractice cases could have been prevented by greater attention to the details of good diagnosis and treatment, careful record keeping, and *better communication* between doctor and patient, and between doctor and doctor.

Society can become too sophisticated, too technology oriented and, in the process, also become too impersonal about those matters that should be highly personal and based on one-on-one relationships. We all know the frustrations of trying to correct a billing error when a com-

[1] From the keynote address delivered by Chief Justice Warren Burger at the National Conference on the Causes of Popular Dissatisfaction with the Administration of Justice, St. Paul, Minnesota, April 1976.

puter seems to stand between human and human. The costs, not only in terms of understanding and empathy but in terms of real money, can be staggering. Premiums paid by doctors for malpractice insurance in 1976 were estimated to total about $1.5 *billion,* up from $60 million in 1960 and $370 million in 1970. They are likely to exceed $3 *billion* per year before the 1980s are behind us. In 1976, California doctors were presented with a 376 *percent* increase over 1975 in premiums for their protective insurance. In 1982, the carriers for doctors in southern Florida proposed an average 358 percent increase in malpractice insurance premiums, raising the required premium for a general surgeon to as much as $66,000 *per year,* and $80,000 for a high-risk specialty such as neurosurgery. These costs, of course, eventually appear in the cost of health-care services regardless of who pays the bill.

Many private insurance carriers will no longer write policies for medical malpractice insurance. In an ever-increasing number of states, the only protection available to doctors is through doctor-owned malpractice insurance companies that operate like cooperatives. Even though they are strictly not-for-profit, they find themselves in a constant loss spiral with resultant large increases in premiums from year to year as pay-out far exceeds income. Eventually, the situation may go totally out of control. Malpractice insurance will no longer be available for any price, much as crime insurance is not available in certain high-crime areas or flood insurance in designated "flood plain" regions. Then the truly wronged and injured patient might obtain whatever judgments the courts saw fit to render, but actual recovery of money would be limited to what the defendant doctor had: personal assets. Few doctors own assets anything like the multimillions bandied about by courts these days, and such judgments would cease to be meaningful. At the bottom line, how much could you buy with an uncollectable judgment or one in which the defendant, the doctor against whom you won the case, only actually owned assets with a value equal to 5 percent of your "judgment."

The budget for operation of the Food and Drug Administration for 1982 was about $350 million for some 7,000 employees. Of this, it is estimated that around $135 million was spent on regulatory activities involving human drugs, medical devices, and biological products (vaccines).

Still to be counted, but defying estimation, are the costs of the judicial process for malpractice lawsuits, the majority of which are considered to be without merit by the very people executing them.

Compensation for injuries is entirely just, and the right to seek compensation appropriate to the injury must be protected. But frivolous malpractice suits make no sense whatsoever and cause costly and irreparable damage to all involved: patient, physician, attorney, court, and government.

The quality of medical care is not necessarily improving but deteriorating as a result of the malpractice crisis. You, the patient, are receiving less effective and less empathetic care from your physician because of his or her ever-present concern about a lawsuit. Your costs are enormously increased by your doctor's defensive actions and by the escalating cost of malpractice litigation, those cases with merit that are won as well as those without merit that are dropped or lost. You no longer trust your doctor, and as a result fail to receive the comfort that would otherwise have been yours. Your doctor's gratification from practicing medicine is being diminished, and the nature of the profession in the future will be decidedly different. Fewer devoted and dedicated young people will want to enter this profession, or at least that part of it that concerns itself with patient care as the principal activity. An ever-increasing number of individuals motivated primarily by the promise of financial reward may be tomorrow's doctors, and medical practice will truly become a "business" rather than just a dedicated professional endeavor that uses sound business practices. Continuing education for the practicing physician is increasing greatly, but it still reaches mainly those doctors who were always sincerely concerned with keeping up and rarely touches those who need it most. Additional malpractice litigation does not seem to change this significantly.

A better relationship with your doctor, on the other hand, is not dependent on outside forces, consumer activism, legislative bodies, or the judicial system. Rather, it is a highly personal thing involving, really, only two people: you and your doctor, with scarcely a smattering of outside influence from nurses, assistants, technicians, and receptionists. How good or how bad this relationship is, remains, or becomes is up to you and to your doctor and requires a good deal of understanding and empathy on the part of both. Like a marriage, this relationship can become rather intimate, and like a marriage, it requires nurturing and compromise from both sides. It can break down and fail, too, like a marriage, with some of the same kind of pain.

Still, it makes more sense to maintain a good relationship whenever possible and to end it when necessary rather than to go on in a mutually hostile and uncomfortable atmosphere. There is neither substitute nor monetary compensation for the benefits of a good patient–doctor union, and antagonism on the part of either impedes the good that can be done or received. In short, it simply makes no sense and produces no "winners." The satisfaction that compensates the physician for his strenuous and demanding life is denied him, and the care and comfort needed by the patient is likewise aborted. I do not know who first jumped on the carousel of mutual distrust and set it into motion, but I do recognize clearly that if two people *are* on a playground carousel and one is pushing while the other is dragging his foot on the ground, it will not operate very efficiently.

Patients must understand that doctors are people, and doctors must recall that patients are people. The world we live in is different in many ways from that of a generation ago, and among those changes to which we must adapt are the facts that doctors no longer make house calls or work eighteen-hour days and patients no longer view doctors with all-trusting awe. A little has been lost by these changes, but much has been gained as well. The technological advances of the last two decades are nothing short of mind boggling. We should try to recognize the old good and the new good and benefit from them without dwelling on those aspects of doctor–patient relationships that have fallen into disuse.

Intimately involved in the relationship, in which malpractice litigation represents the total breakdown akin to divorce litigation for a marriage, are the intermediate steps, the recognition by the doctor and the exercise by the patient of rights. Open and honest communication will include full disclosure of information to the patient and participation by the patient in an intelligent manner in the decision-making process, in the selection of treatment to be administered. The doctor must learn to accept and welcome the patient's participation in what was formerly the physician's prerogative. At the same time, the patient, having demanded that participation, must step cautiously when "blaming" the doctor afterward if the joint decision produces less than wholly satisfactory results.

Are we heading in that direction? Probably, but via a devious and tiresome route. The problem of malpractice lawsuits is by no means restricted to the medical profession. Attorneys are becoming truly concerned by a steady increase in *legal* malpractice suits instituted by former clients alleging professional incompetence or negligence. Dentists have been "touched" as well. Perhaps the ultimate absurdity—or a logical extension, depending on your point of view—is *clergy* malpractice, now a problem real enough to have resulted in the availability and the purchase of malpractice insurance by clergy, especially where they engage in counseling activities.

The first such case to become widely publicized, and which is acknowledged to have brought the problem and the concern home to the profession, involved a wife who went to her pastor for help regarding marital difficulties. In the course of the counseling, the clergyman suggested a trial separation. When the woman informed her husband, he became so enraged he got his gun and shot her. She recovered and sued the pastor for clergy malpractice! In another widely publicized action, the parents of a suicide victim sued the pastor who had been counseling their son for failing to recognize in him a serious psychiatric disorder and refer him for more expert care.

Norman Cousins, well-known author, in his book *Anatomy of an Illness* (Boston: G. K. Hall, 1980), wrote:

> The terrifying fear of malpractice suits drives many doctors to tell the worst. If it happens, they have performed faultlessly, if not, they're heroes. And that's too bad because hope is not just an abstraction. It is one of the leading activators of the body's healing system.

Dr. Robert S. Mendelsohn, author of *Confessions of a Medical Heretic* (Chicago: Contemporary Books, 1979), told us:

> The Old Testament instructs doctors to discuss the next day's menu with a dying patient so as not to remove hope. A fetish of modern medicine is complete candor so doctors lie when they shouldn't and don't when they should . . . They say, "Trust me," because they think you're too stupid to understand and if you did you wouldn't take the cure.

In *The Making of a Surgeon* (New York: Random House, 1976), Dr. William A. Nolen declared:

> Most doctors tell the truth most of the time. However, I don't think they are obligated to tell the patient, aside from his next of kin, more than he needs to know, unless he specifically asks.
>
> The most unforgivable inadequacy of the doctor as human being is when, by attitude and diminished interest, he places distance between himself and a patient he has concluded is hopeless.

When I am subjected to tales of supposed or real medical abuses at social functions, I always ask if the individual still uses the same doctor. If the answer is "yes," I have little sympathy for the person.

If two persons are to have any kind of working relationship in which mutual benefit is to be realized, they must develop mutual respect, and they must communicate with each other to relate expectations and to declare dissatisfactions. If they do neither, the relationship is doomed from the outset, and if it should manage to survive for a while with intensive care, it is certainly far from satisfying to either participant, and the objectives, if achieved at all, are tainted and less than ideal. It may take more effort to communicate than to complain, but the results are worth it. Then the courts could spend their time addressing *really* important matters like that business of the neighbor's dog who is allowed to run loose and keeps eating your rosebuds.

Some of the topics being tossed around in medical–legal circles these days as likely to be the malpractice issues of the near future include:

1. Physicians' reluctance to refer patients to other doctors more expert in the area of a given disease;
2. Physicians' reluctance to get together for a personal discussion about a patient whose care they share;

3. Psychiatrists' liability if the psychiatrists know a patient is suicidal and if the patient does, in fact, commit suicide. Since the most expert psychiatrists admit it is virtually impossible to predict which patient will just talk about it or will actually attempt suicide, it appears that the fine line between baby-sitting and psychiatric care is about to be dimmed.

4. Increased efforts to hold doctors financially responsible for the care and raising of unwanted children under the doctrine of "wrongful birth" when vasectomies, tube-tying, or abortions fail to prevent pregnancy or the birth of a full-term child.

5. Psychiatrists' liability for "wrongful death" of third parties, i.e., people about whom the psychiatrist's patient exhibited or admitted fantasies and/or desires to harm. Suddenly the confidentiality of the psychiatrist's couch is made secondary to his or her responsibility to warn everyone about whom the patient fantasizes. Undoubtedly the murder of John Lennon and the attempted assassination of President Reagan will lend weight to this rather bizarre direction of medical liability. At least two cases, one in California and one in New Jersey, have been decided within the confines of this new doctrine.

6. A move to permit patients to recover damages from doctors on the basis of "outrageous behavior," more or less defined as intentional or reckless conduct marked by knowing disregard of likely consequences other than physical injury to the patient. One of the early cases involved the team doctor for a professional football club who falsely reported to a sportswriter that a particular player had a fatal illness when, in fact, the player had merely decided to retire after suffering one injury too many for his liking.

New Jersey recently put into effect a new system of effecting hospital charges for insurance purposes known as "Diagnosis Related Groupings (DRG)." This system establishes flat fees for hospital patients according to their DRG, but irrespective of the actual care rendered or the length of the stay. Thus a patient kept overnight for a fractured toe, then released with a splint, will trigger the same hospital bill as a patient kept for ten days because of a more major fracture in the same Diagnosis Related Grouping.

A patient was admitted to the hospital via the emergency room with complaints of dizziness and headache. The physician in charge of the case requested a consultation with a neurologist, a tentative diagnosis of viral encephalitis was made, and special spinal fluid studies to confirm it were recommended. Acting in accordance with his responsibility under the DRG rules, the hospital pathologist denied the request for these special and rather expensive tests, which had to be sent to an outside laboratory because the hospital's own facilities could not perform them. The patient later died without a firm diagnosis being established. The pathologist's reasoning was that the hospital would be paid the same fee with or without these tests, and his responsibility under the DRG rules and the Health Care Facilities Act was to contain costs wherever possible.

The patient's widow has brought an action for "wrongful death" against the attending physician, the consulting neurologist, and the hospital itself.

The attending physician was sued on the basis that he had a duty to exercise the degree of care, knowledge, and skill expected of doctors of similar circumstances and should have pursued the matter and seen that the tests were carried out. The neurologist was named a defendant on the same basis, but since he *did* render a satisfactory level of care—he examined the patient, made a tentative diagnosis, and recommended confirmatory tests—it is likely that he will not be held liable for subsequent injuries. The hospital was named under the doctrine of *respondeat superior*, the responsibility of the boss, or freely translated, "The Buck Stops Here." Since the pathologist was an employee of the hospital and made his decision in accordance with alleged hospital policy, the doctrine says the hospital should be held responsible for his acts.

Something is wrong with a system in which those who attempt to comply with state law and state regulations are exposed to liability for malpractice by reason of their efforts to do so.

When a problem such as medical malpractice is discussed by a member of the group against which such suits are filed, ulterior motives may well be suspected, though I have tried to be fair and impartial in my evaluations and discussions. But when concern is expressed by those who profit from the situation but are equally disturbed by the unfairness of it all, it is time to stop and take notice.

A group of lawyers and doctors recently announced the formation of an interprofessional organization called Lawyers Protecting People from Malicious and Unjustified Lawsuits, Inc. The president, a Florida trial attorney, said the new group was designed to reduce the increasing number of nuisance cases being filed nationwide by suing lawyers who filed unfounded and malicious suits. Its primary goal is to represent doctors, other members of the health professions, and police officers, all of whom are frequently the victims of lawsuits without probable cause.

Now *there's* a howdy do!

APPENDICES

1. A REPRESENTATIVE SAMPLE OF
AN INFORMED-CONSENT FORM

(NOTE: This form is presented only as an example. If you are asked to sign a form that differs from this, it does not mean that it is wrong, incorrect, illegal, or unsatisfactory. There are many roads to Rome and many ways to obtain informed consent. Consult the discussion in Chapter 4 for advice on how to assure yourself that you are giving consent that is truly "informed").

I (*name of patient*) hereby grant to Dr. (*his or her name*) and/or his associates, Drs. (*name of other doctors who may be in a joint practice, group practice, partnership or professional corporation or medical group and who usually share patient responsibility, especially during off hours*), or such other doctors, nurses, technicians, or other paramedical personnel authorized to act under my doctor's supervision or at his direction my consent to perform (*common name of diagnostic test or surgical procedure*) on me.

The doctor has explained to me and I fully understand the nature of the test or procedure to be done, and he has answered to my satisfaction any questions I had about it. I understand that this procedure involves certain risks, and the risks have been explained to my satisfaction. I also understand that if I refuse this procedure, it could be dangerous to my health and well-being, and these risks as well have been explained to me. I also understand that any medical, diagnostic, or surgical procedure carries with it some unexpected risks that cannot be predicted or explained in advance.

Furthermore, I understand that there are other tests, procedures, or treatments that could be used for my condition. The reasons the doctor has selected this one as the one he considers most suitable for me have been explained to my satisfaction.

I and my doctor agree that he will not do anything beyond the scope of this consent without consulting with me further, unless such delay would significantly endanger my health or my life. If in his opinion any attempt to consult with me further would place me in even greater risk, then I authorize him to do what he considers necessary for my immediate welfare to prevent serious disability or even loss of my life.

Date

Signature of patient (or parent or guardian when applicable)

Signatures of witnesses. (*Ideally, they should be persons not directly involved with the procedure. In other words,* not *the doctor or doctors named in the consent.*)

2. THE RIGHTS OF PATIENTS:
A SAMPLE BILL

ASSEMBLY, No. 464

STATE OF NEW JERSEY

PRE-FILED FOR INTRODUCTION
IN THE 1982 SESSION

By Assemblyman WOLF, Assemblywoman GARVIN,
Assemblyman PATERNITI, Assemblywoman
MUHLER, Assemblymen FRANKS, VILLANE,
BENNETT and WEIDEL

AN ACT concerning the rights of patients in general
hospitals.

1 BE IT ENACTED *by the Senate and General Assembly*
2 *of the State of New Jersey:*
1 1. The Legislature finds and declares that a person
2 admitted to a general hospital may feel overwhelmed
3 and uncertain as to his condition and course of treat-
4 ment, and that a declaration of a bill of rights for hos-
5 pital patients may lead to fuller understanding and
6 greater security on the part of patients as well as to
7 greater sensitivity in the provision of medical care.
1 2. Every person admitted to a general hospital as
2 licensed by the State Department of Health pursuant
3 to P. L. 1971, c. 136 (C. 26:2II–1 et seq.) shall have
4 the right:

5   a. To considerate and respectful care;

6   b. To be informed, upon request, of the name of the
7 physician responsible for coordinating his care;

8   c. To obtain from the physician complete, current
9 information concerning his diagnosis, treatment, and
10 prognosis in terms he can reasonably be expected to
11 understand. When it is not medically advisable to give
12 this information to the patient, it shall be made avail-
13 able to another person on his behalf;

14   d. To receive from the physician information neces-
15 sary to give informed consent prior to the start of any
16 procedure or treatment and which, except for those
17 emergency situations not requiring an informed con-
18 sent, shall include as a minimum the specific procedure
19 or treatment, the medically significant risks involved,
20 and the possible duration of incapacitation, if any. The
21 patient shall be advised of any medically significant
22 alternatives for care or treatment;

23   e. To refuse treatment to the extent permitted by
24 law and to be informed of the medical consequences
25 of this action;

26   f. To privacy to the extent consistent with providing
27 adequate medical care to the patient. This shall not
28 preclude discussion of a patient's case or examination
29 of a patient by appropriate health care personnel;

30   g. To privacy and confidentiality of all records per-
31 taining to his treatment, except as otherwise provided
32 by law or third party payment contract;

33   h. To expect that within its capacity, the hospital
34 will make reasonable response to his request for services;

35   i. To be informed by the physician of any continu-
36 ing health care requirements which may follow dis-
37 charge;

38   j. To be informed by the hospital of the necessity of
39 transfer to another facility prior to the transfer and of
40 any alternatives to it which may exist;

41   k. To be informed, upon request, of other health
42 care and educational institutions that the hospital has
43 authorized to participate in his treatment;
44   l. To be advised if the hospital proposes to engage
45 in or perform human research or experimentation and
46 to refuse to participate in these projects;
47   m. To examine and receive an explanation of his
48 bill, regardless of source of payment;
49   n. To be advised of the hospital rules and regulations
50 that apply to his conduct as a patient; and,
51   o. To treatment without discrimination as to race,
52 age, religion, sex, national origin, or source of payment.
1   3. The administrator of a general hospital shall in-
2 sure that a written notice of the rights set forth in this
3 act be given to the patient or his guardian upon ad-
4 mittance to the hospital and to each individual already
5 in residence. The administrator shall also post this notice
6 in a conspicuous public place in the hospital.
1   4. A patient whose rights as defined herein are vio-
2 lated shall have a cause of action against the person
3 committing the violation. The Department of Health
4 may initiate an action in the name of the State to en-
5 force the provisions of this act and any rules or regula-
6 tions promulgated pursuant to this act. The action may
7 be brought in any court of competent jurisdiction to
8 enforce such rights and to recover actual and punitive
9 damages for their violation. Any plaintiff who prevails
10 in any action shall be entitled to recover reasonable
11 attorney's fees and costs of the action.
1   5. The Commissioner of Health is authorized to
2 adopt rules and regulations in accordance with the
3 provisions of the "Administrative Procedure Act," P. L.
4 1968, c. 410 (C. 52:14B–1 et seq.) to effectuate the
5 provisions and purposes of this act.
1   6. This act shall take effect on the ninetieth day
2 following enactment.

STATEMENT

Very often, a person admitted to a general hospital for the treatment of an injury or illness may feel overwhelmed and uncertain. The anxiety and stress that accompanies a serious or painful physical condition may be increased by the unfamiliar surroundings and new situations with which the individual must now deal. As a result, rather than asking for complete and accurate information vital to his situation, a patient may find himself reticent to appropriately question hospital personnel.

This bill establishes a bill of rights for persons receiving care in a general hospital and is an attempt to clarify for the patient what he can legitimately expect from hospital staff as well as what his own responsibilities may be. The administrator of the hospital must see to it that a written notice of these rights be given to each patient when he is admitted and also that the notice be posted in a conspicuous public place in the facility. The promulgation and dissemination of this bill of rights for hospital patients will hopefully contribute to more effective patient care and greater satisfaction for the patient, his physician, and the hospital organization.

3. MEDICAL MALPRACTICE: SAMPLE PROCEDURES

RULE 4:21. PROFESSIONAL LIABILITY CLAIMS AGAINST MEMBERS OF MEDICAL PROFESSION; PROCEDURE

Ed. Note: Former Rules 4:21 1 to 4:21 10 have been deleted and replaced, effective September 11, 1978, by Rules 4:21 1 to 4:21 7 set forth herein.

4:21–1. Purpose of Rule

The procedure set forth in R. 4:21 is for the common interest of the public, the medical and legal professions in the processing of medical malpractice actions with the view toward discouraging baseless actions and encouraging settlement of those actions based on reasonable medical probability; to monitor efficiently these cases through the court; and, to assist in the early disposition of medical malpractice actions.

Note: Adopted July 24, 1978 to be effective September 11, 1978.

4:21–2. Processing of Medical Malpractice Cases

(a) **Caption of Action.** A medical malpractice action shall be so designated in the caption and be given a special identifying letter by the clerk.

(b) **Judicial Assignment.** The Assignment Judge shall, whenever feasible, designate one judge before whom all medical malpractice cases in his vicinage shall be pretried. The judge so designated shall preside at all pretrial discovery proceedings, pretrial conference and the hearing set forth herein but shall not preside at the trial of the action.

(c) **Pretrial Conference.** The court shall conduct a pretrial conference pursuant to R. 4:21 1 not later than twelve months following service of process upon the defendants. The pretrial order shall provide for the submission of the claim to a panel as the Courts shall select a substitute in accordance with the provisions herein.

(c) **Time for Hearing.** When an acceptable panel is constituted, the presiding judge shall fix the time and place for hearing. All applications for adjournment shall be made to the presiding judge.

Note: Adopted July 24, 1978 to be effective September 11, 1978.

4:21–5. Hearing Before Panel; Findings; Effect

(a) **Participation at Hearing; Confidentiality.** The hearing shall be informal and without a stenographic record.

Except as otherwise provided in this section, no statement or expression of opinion made in the course of the hearing shall be admissible in evidence either as an admission or otherwise in any trial of the action. If any of the parties to the hearing fails to appear or to comply with the rules set forth herein respecting the hearing, the presiding judge may enter such order as justice requires.

(b) **Presentation of Facts.** The parties shall set forth their factual and legal contentions in any of the following forms: narrative statement, question and answer, written statement, sworn testimony, or in such other form as the panel deems appropriate. On application by any party, the presiding judge may issue subpoenas and compel compliance therewith in accordance with the appropriate provisions of Rule 1:9 (Subpoenas). All witnesses and parties called to testify may be cross-examined by any adverse party, subject to the discretion of the presiding judge. The parties shall submit all written material including the original or copies of all hospital records and other reports upon which they shall rely to the members of the panel no later than ten (10) days prior to the hearing by filing same with the presiding judge.

(c) **Scope of Panel Jurisdiction.** The parties to the hearing may, at any time, enter into stipulations concerning procedure and evidence and may agree to extend the jurisdiction of the panel to determine damages. Co-defendants in the action who are not doctors may submit to such hearing and thereby become subject to the same rights and sanctions affecting the plaintiff and defendant doctor or doctors.

(d) **Expert Witness.** The panel may request an additional doctor having particular expertise in the specialty involved to assist it in the determination of the claim. Such doctor shall make a report to the panel. The panel shall determine the fee and expenses to be paid to such doctor and the parties to the hearing shall share equally in such fee and expense. This doctor and the doctor member of the panel may be called at subsequent trial of the action as a witness by any of the parties. The party calling such witness at trial shall pay all reasonable fees and expenses of the doctor.

(e) **Findings; Admissibility at Trial.** At the conclusion of the hearing, the panel shall make specific findings of fact as to each hereinafter provided and shall prescribe a schedule for further processing of the panel hearing.

Note: Adopted July 24, 1978 to be effective September 11, 1978.

4:21–3. Panel Members: Doctors and Lawyers

For purposes of Rule 4:21, the Administrative Director of the Courts shall maintain the following panels: (1) a panel of doctors designated by the Medical Society of New Jersey; (2) a panel of doctors designated by the New Jersey Society of Osteopathic Physicians and Surgeons; and (3) a panel of attorneys with trial experience designated by the Supreme Court. Additions or deletions may be made to these panels at any time at the discretion of the Administrative Director of the Courts.

Note: Adopted July 24, 1978 to be effective September 11, 1978.

4:21–4. Appointment of Panel; Notification and Disqualification

(a) **Appointment of Panel.** All hearings shall be held before a panel consisting of a judge who shall preside as chairman, a doctor and an attorney, all of whom shall be appointed in accordance with the following provisions.

(1) The chairman shall be the same judge to whom the action has been assigned pursuant to R. 4:21–2(b) unless

the Assignment Judge, in extraordinary circumstances and for good cause shown, otherwise orders.

(2) The doctor shall be selected by the Administrative Director of the Courts from the medical or osteopathic panel, as appropriate, depending upon the discipline of the defendant doctor or doctors. Where practicable, the doctor panelist shall be a practitioner in the field of specialty involved in the case.

(3) The attorney shall be selected by the Administrative Director of the Courts.

(b) **Notification and Disqualification.** The Administrative Director of the Courts shall notify the doctor and attorney that they have been selected to be members of a panel for a particular case and shall request that they disclose any circumstances likely to create a presumption of bias or which they believe might otherwise disqualify them. Information disclosed in response to such a request shall then be forwarded to all parties together with notification to all parties of the identity of the panel members. Within fifteen days after mailing of notification of the panel selection to all parties, any party may file and serve within objection to the designation of the doctor or attorney, with supporting reasons therefor. This objection shall be heard by the judge presiding as chairman of the panel. Copies of the written objection and the judicial determination thereon shall be sent to the Administrative Director of the Courts. Whenever a panelist is disqualified, the Administrative Director of the Courts shall select a substitute in accordance with the provisions herein.

(c) **Time for Hearing.** When an acceptable panel is constituted, the presiding judge shall fix the time and place for hearing. All applications for adjournment shall be made to the presiding judge.

Note: Adopted July 24, 1978 to be effective September 11, 1978.

4:21–5. Hearing Before Panel; Findings; Effect

(a) **Participation at Hearing; Confidentiality.** The hearing shall be informal and without a stenographic record. Except as otherwise provided in this section, no statement or expression of opinion made in the course of the hearing shall be admissible in evidence either as an admission or otherwise in any trial of the action. If any of the parties to the hearing fails to appear or to comply with the rules set forth herein respecting the hearing, the presiding judge may enter such order as justice requires.

(b) **Presentation of Facts.** The parties shall set forth their factual and legal contentions in any of the following forms: narrative statement, question and answer, written statement, sworn testimony, or in such other form as the panel deems appropriate. On application by any party, the presiding judge may issue subpoenas and compel compliance therewith in accordance with the appropriate provisions of Rule 1:9 (Subpoenas). All witnesses and parties called to testify may be cross-examined by any adverse party, subject to the discretion of the presiding judge. The parties shall submit all written material including the original or copies of all hospital records and other reports upon which they shall rely to the members of the panel no later than ten (10) days prior to the hearing by filing same with the presiding judge.

(c) **Scope of Panel Jurisdiction.** The parties to the hearing may, at any time, enter into stipulations concerning procedure and evidence and may agree to extend the jurisdiction of the panel to determine damages. Co-defendants in the action who are not doctors may submit to such hearing and thereby become subject to the same rights and sanctions affecting the plaintiff and defendant doctor or doctors.

(d) **Expert Witness.** The panel may request an additional doctor having particular expertise in the specialty involved to assist it in the determination of the claim. Such doctor shall make a report to the panel. The panel shall determine the fee and expenses to be paid to such doctor and the parties to the hearing shall share equally in such fee and expense. This doctor and the doctor member of the panel may be called at subsequent trial of the action as a witness by any of the parties. The party calling such witness at trial shall pay all reasonable fees and expenses of the doctor.

(e) **Findings; Admissibility at Trial.** At the conclusion of the hearing, the panel shall make specific findings of fact as to each medical issue and an appropriate order determining whether the claim is based on reasonable medical probability shall be served on all parties to the action. This order shall be filed and sealed in accordance with R. 4:21–7 with full restrictions as to all parties and their attorneys against disclosure. If the order setting forth the panel's disposition is unanimous, the findings contained therein shall be admissible in evidence at trial upon the request of any party to the hearing. The recommendation shall not be binding upon the jury or upon a judge sitting as the trier of the facts, but shall be accorded such weight as the jury or the judge sitting as the trier of the facts chooses to ascribe to it in view of all the relevant evidence adduced at trial.

(f) **Documents; Identification; Disposition.** All writings as defined in Evidence Rule 1(13) upon which the parties rely at the hearing shall be marked for identification and shall be returned to the respective parties after entry of the order.

(g) **Participation of Panel Members in Trial.** The judge presiding at the hearing shall not preside at the trial, nor shall any panel member participate in the trial either as counsel or witness except as otherwise provided herein.

Note: Adopted July 24, 1978 to be effective September 11, 1978.

4:21–6. Rehearing

The panel by majority vote of its members may grant a single rehearing, but such rehearing shall not be granted solely because the plaintiff or defendant doctor or doctors has substituted counsel.

Note: Adopted July 24, 1978 to be effective September 11, 1978.

4:21–7. Proceedings to be in Camera; Secrecy

All proceedings, records, findings and recommendations of the panel shall be confidential and shall not be used in any proceeding other than the trial of the action. All proceedings shall be in camera and no records shall be made thereof.

Note: Adopted July 24, 1978 to be effective September 11, 1978.

COMMENT

R. 4:21 as adopted as part of the 1969 revision provided a mechanism for the voluntary pretrial submission by plaintiffs or potential plaintiffs of medical malpractice claims to medical-legal panels. This rule was eliminated effective September 11, 1978 and replaced with R. 4:21–1 to 4:21–7, inclusive, providing, in essence, for mandatory pretrial panel review in this category of negligence actions.

The impetus and justification for the substantial practice change represented by the 1978 version of R. 4:21 is explicated and analyzed in the Report of the Supreme Court's Committee on Relations with the Medical Profession, 101 N.J.L.J., Index page 45 (1978). Essentially, it was the Committee's conclusion that the voluntary submission mechanism had completely failed in its purpose of expediting disposition of medical malpractice cases by screening out of the system those lacking in merit and encouraging the settlement of those which were well-founded. It was the Committee's further conclusion that these purposes would be met by the proposed mechanism set forth in these rules, the primary features of which are assignment of a single judge in each vicinage to preside during the entire pretrial procedure; the conduct of a pretrial conference within 12 months following service of process; the mandatory submission of the matter following the pretrial to a 3-member panel consisting of the pretrial judge, a doctor and a lawyer; detailed provisions for the conduct of the panel hearing and significantly the admissibility in evidence at the trial itself of the recommendation of the panel, providing it is unanimous. The rule further provides for the confidentiality of the panel hearing which is required to be held in camera and no record thereof to be made. The Committee's minority report (101 N.J.L.J. at 452) dissented only in respect of the admissibility of the panel's recommendation.

As a historical matter Marsello v. Barnett, 50 N.J. 577 (1967), reviewing the history and intent of the former rules and holding that either party was free to withdraw his consent to the hearing at any time before the commencement of the hearing, although a party making a late withdrawal of consent might be chargeable (after the trial verdict) with his adversary's actual expenses in preparing for the hearing. A party was not, however, permitted to withdraw his consent after the panel had decided against him. Grove v. Seltzer, 56 N.J. 321 (1970).

4. MEDICAL MALPRACTICE VERDICTS, CALIFORNIA SUPERIOR COURT, 1972–1980

Year	Total No. of Verdicts	In Favor of Defendant	In Favor of Plaintiff	Total Amount Awarded	Average Award
1972	137	60%	40%	$11,016,305	$200,296
1973	165	70%	30%	$10,642,391	$212,848
1974	215	66%	34%	$9,768,628	$133,817
1975	215	73%	27%	$9,025,248	$152,970
1976	226	74%	26%	$9,661,795	$166,582
1977	205	71%	29%	$16,066,354	$272,311
1978	204	72%	28%	$11,456,873	$200,998
1979	204	65%	35%	$24,961,427	$351,569
1980	180	61%	39%	$21,607,739	$308,682

Source: The Insurance Information Institute of California, as reported in *The Journal of the Medical Society of New Jersey*, Vol. 78, No. 10, September 1981.

Notes:
1. California has one of the highest rates of malpractice suits filed and won against the doctor.
2. It is interesting to note the actual percentage of cases won by the plaintiff (the patient) and that won by the defendant (the doctor).
3. These figures do not include lawsuits filed but which never result in a courtroom verdict. These include cases withdrawn at some point because of a lack of merit as well as cases settled out of court.
4. The total amount awarded, plus all sums paid in out-of-court settlements, represents money paid out by the insurance carriers, which, in turn, is reflected in the premiums they charge, which, eventually, shows up in the fees of all doctors, not just those who lost cases and had judgments entered against them.

5. "WOULD YOU BELIEVE . . . ?"

A sampling of malpractice cases filed within the past few years, extraordinary enough to have received widespread publicity in newspapers or professional newsletters. Some describe disgraceful examples of negligence, while others simply make you sit and scratch your head in wonderment.

A New Jersey case, brought to the State Court of Appeals, was lost by a couple who sued their doctor for performing a different type of sterilization operation on the wife than the one he had described to her. The operation was unsuccessful, and she subsequently became pregnant and bore a healthy child, only to sue the surgeon for the costs of raising the child to the age of legal majority on the grounds of "Wrongful Birth." The Court ruled that a patient cannot sue to recover the costs of raising "an unwanted child," as the suit alleged. Bear in mind that the basis of the suit was *not* the lack of informed consent for the "other" sterilization procedure, or even for the fact that it failed. There have been similar cases filed against pharmacists on the basis of their having misread or misinterpreted prescriptions for birth control pills and dispensed something else, with unexpected pregnancies as an unfortunate result. Some states have allowed this claim.

A twenty-five-year-old Colorado man sued his mother for "parental malpractice" (is there any end to it?), alleging "intentional infliction of emotional distress." The suit was thrown out by a judge who ruled that it was wholly without merit, whereupon the mother then sued the son's psychiatrist, contending that the doctor had encouraged the son's suit and thus held her up to nationwide ridicule.

A Manhattan federal judge told a California woman that she could not collect damages on her twin sister's death in a plane crash merely because she said she had "ESP empathy" (the words used in the lawsuit) and shared the pain. The judge ruled that she would have had to have actually been present—the pain-sharing between twins is a documented phenomenon—but could not collect when the crash occurred in the Canary Islands while the suing sister was in California.

A New Jersey couple won a suit against a world-renowned New York City medical center because of negligence in monitoring their four-and-a-half-year-old daughter in the intensive-care unit following emergency surgery to correct a birth defect in her heart. The temporary deprivation of oxygen to the brain led to severe brain damage, and the child "will have to be fed, groomed, dressed, and bathed by others for the rest of her life." The court awarded them $30,000 a year plus 4 percent interest until the child dies or reaches age seventy. If she survives to seventy, the award would total $11 million.

A former New Jersey couple who gave birth to a child later diagnosed as suffering from cystic fibrosis sued the doctor who had failed to diagnose it during the first five years of the child's life, at which time the mother conceived a second time. The couple alleged they would not have had a second child had they known, and the court ruled that if the second child was also born with cystic fibrosis, the doctor would be liable for all of its medical care.

A nineteen-year-old man won $2.5 million dollars in a malpractice award against the State of New Jersey for having kept him in a school for the mentally retarded following a diagnosis by the family doctor, when in fact his problem was *deafness*. He alleged, successfully, that he was admitted to the state hospital for mentally defective children in 1965 and was held there until 1972 without a single reevaluation by the staff.

A Brooklyn, New York, man sued a surgeon, claiming a bungled lung operation had made him short of breath and ruined his sex life. He was awarded $1 million.

A California man won a case against his physician for "mental and emotional stress" when his wife was misdiagnosed as having syphilis, an action that eventually led to the couple's divorce. The California Supreme Court ruled that one could recover damages for emotional distress unaccompanied by physical injury, a new legal concept not previously permitted.

In New York City, an ex-model was awarded $800,000 on her claim that she became addicted to certain painkilling drugs. It was believed to be the first time a jury made a malpractice award for drug addiction based on the action of doctors. The suit had alleged that the pain that necessitated the medication resulted from improper diagnosis and treatment of her back ailment.

An obstetrician and an anesthesiologist were sued by the parents of a child who suffers from cerebral palsy because of alleged errors on the part of the doctors that cut off the oxygen supply of the baby during birth. An incorrect dose of a labor-inducing drug was blamed for unusually severe contractions. The award was $7.5 million. In another case, a seven-year-old New York City girl who suffered brain damage at birth because of a lack of oxygen was the recipient of an out-of-court settlement of $3,500 per month, increasing by 3 percent each year. Her lawyers calculated that if she lives to be seventy-two, the current average life expectancy for females, the total she will have received will be about $23 million.

A thirty-seven-year-old New Jersey man sued three doctors and a hospital, asking $53 million for alleged surgical malpractice in which an attempt to cut the nerves to an injured arm to relieve pain was made. The suit alleged that the doctors discovered they had cut the nerves in the wrong arm, paralyzing it. Upon the realization that it was the wrong arm, they went ahead and severed the nerves in the other arm as well without consulting the patient, thus leaving him without the use of either arm. This case illustrates both negligence and proceeding without consent of the patient, who might very well have elected, after the error was made known, to remain with the pain and the use of at least one arm.

In a New York case, a dentist had been accused and convicted of sexually abusing one of his female patients. The woman then sought to collect $16 million in damages from the dentist's malpractice insurance, but the court rejected the claim, stating that the dentist's actions went beyond the scope of his malpractice coverage and the insurance carrier was not liable.

A seventeen-year-old Pennsylvania woman became unconscious at a party. CPR was attempted but failed to revive her, and she died several hours later. Autopsy revealed significant levels of a barbiturate sleeping pill in her blood, and the Commonwealth of Pennsylvania charged her doctor with involuntary manslaughter, alleging that the death was a direct result of the reckless and grossly negligent manner in which he had prescribed the sleeping pill. The doctor was sentenced to one to three years in prison, fined $5,000, and required to pay the costs of the prosecution. Though this case is too new to know what followed the conviction, it is highly likely that a malpractice suit was probably filed by the girl's family subsequent to the criminal conviction. It would not be hard to win it.

Acting on appeal of a suit filed by an individual confined in a mental institution from 1957 to the early seventies at the instigation of his father, who thought his son was suffering "delusions," the Supreme Court declared that it would be a denial of due process of law for a state to order confinement of the mentally ill solely for the purpose of treating them if the person were not deemed to be a danger either to himself or to others. The original case in the Fifth Circuit Court in Florida had awarded the patient both compensatory and punitive damages by reason of the state having deprived him of his liberty, and this was upheld by higher courts.

A naval veteran treated at a VA hospital for injuries received in a 1975 motorcycle accident suffered the accidental severing of his sciatic nerve in the course of several operations to rebuild a badly damaged thigh. The physician established that the nerve was so encased in scar tissue and dead tissue that it had become impossible to see. The court ruled that the physician was *not* negligent in having accidentally severed the nerve, but *was* negligent in having failed to obtain the patient's informed consent prior to the surgery, this meaning that he had failed to inform the patient of the possibility that the nerve might be damaged or cut unintentionally during the operation.

A California epileptic was given the customary medications used to control seizures, one of which is often phenobarbital, a sedative. It is usual, and in some states mandatory, for the physician prescribing this medication for continued use to report the facts to either the health department or the commissioner of motor vehicles. In this case, no such report was made, and the patient subsequently had an automobile accident in which he was responsible for killing one person and injuring three others. The physicians involved settled their case before trial by acknowledging liability and paying damages to the victims of the accident.

In New York City, a jury decided a case in favor of the patient and against a major private hospital. The woman was seen three times in the course of five days over the Christmas holiday for a persistent severe headache, each time being sent home with a prescription for a headache remedy. Upon later admission to the hospital, a proper diagnosis of brain hemorrhage was finally made. She was left partially paralyzed, but it was not clearly established that this was a result of the delayed admission. The jury awarded her $10 million. At last report, the judge was considering lowering the award.

A Virginia woman consented to an exploratory operation to seek the cause of unexplained vaginal bleeding, but only on the condition that her own doctor be present at the operation. The surgeon failed to make the necessary arrangements and went ahead without the other doctor being present despite several additional requests by the patient. She sued on the grounds of battery (unauthorized surgery without her consent), the jury agreed, and she was awarded $75,000. Both the verdict and the size of the award were upheld by the Virginia Supreme Court on appeal by the surgeon. There was no allegation of injury to the patient, only the failure to abide by the terms and conditions of her consent.

6. PROPOSED EXPANSION OF NURSES' DUTIES: NEW YORK STATE

This is a brief summary of a bill introduced into the New York legislature in 1982 that proposed the expansion of the professional duties of nurses to include diagnosis and treatment of disease, including the writing of prescriptions.

EXPANDED NURSING PRACTICE ACT (A. 11922)

1. This legislation would allow registered nurses, who are specially trained, to diagnose and treat illness and prescribe certain medications upon the nurse obtaining a written agreement with a physician to furnish back-up care and accept referrals. Under such an arrangement, the nurse would provide ambulatory and primary care, the physician would consult and review her work regularly, and a case would be referred to the physician if it proved to be beyond the nurse's scope. The written agreements would not be required for nurses providing the services in hospitals, health maintenance organizations, and classes of facilities determined by the commissioner of health.
2. Prescription writing authority will be provided for nurse practitioners who can demonstrate completion of thirty hours of approved courses in pharmacology. The authority to prescribe and immunize would be based on review and approval of the nurse practitioner's credentials by a separate prescription advisory committee.
3. Statutory ratios of nurse practitioners who may work with a physician are not required.

7. STATUTES OF LIMITATION

A statute of limitation specifies the maximum time available in which to file a lawsuit for an alleged injury or damage, and the conditions under which it applies. This means a definition of when this time period begins to be counted and usually also specifies how it is to be applied in the case of injuries to minors who would not have the right to sue until they reach the age of majority. Such matters are the privilege of each state to determine, and there is, therefore, no uniform set of rules. In addition, from time to time a state court may reinterpret the statute and give one or the other of its definitions a meaning other than the one subscribed to previously. Thus Table 1 is just a guideline, and specific up-to-date information should be sought from an attorney in your state or the state itself regarding a specific incident.

There are two general ways to count the time allowable for filing a law suit. One starts when the negligent act or the act responsible for the injury *occurs* ("occurrence"), while the other counts from when the results of the negligent act are *discovered* ("discovery"). Table 1 shows which method of counting is applicable in your state.

TABLE 1. STATUTES OF LIMITATION BY STATE

STATE	FROM OCCURRENCE	FROM DISCOVERY
Alabama	2 Years	
Alaska	2 Years	
Arizona	3 Years	
Arkansas	2 Years	
California	3 Years	
Colorado		2 Years
Connecticut		2 Years
Delaware	2 Years	
Florida		2 Years
Georgia	2 Years	
Hawaii		2 Years
Idaho	2 Years	
Illinois		2 Years
Indiana	2 Years	
Iowa		2 Years
Kansas	2 Years	
Kentucky		1 Year
Louisiana	1 Year	
Maine	2 Years	
Maryland	5 Years or 3 Years	

whichever is sooner

STATE	FROM OCCURRENCE		FROM DISCOVERY
Massachusetts	3 Years		
Michigan	2 Years	or	6 Months
	whichever is later		
Minnesota	2 Years		
Mississippi			2 Years
Missouri	2 Years		
Montana	3 Years	or	3 Years
	but no more than 5 years		
	from injury		
Nebraska	2 Years		
Nevada	4 Years		
New Hampshire	2 Years		
New Jersey			2 Years
New Mexico	3 Years		
New York	30 Months		
North Carolina	3 Years		
North Dakota			2 Years
Ohio			1 Year
Oklahoma			2 Years
Oregon			2 Years
Pennsylvania			2 Years
Rhode Island	2 Years		
South Carolina	3 Years	or	3 Years
South Dakota	2 Years		
Tennessee	1 Year		
Texas	2 Years		
Utah			2 Years
Vermont	7 Years		
Virginia	2 Years		
Washington	3 Years		
West Virginia			2 Years
Wisconsin	3 Years		
Wyoming	2 Years		
Dist. of Columbia			3 Years

Where the injury has occurred to a minor, many states allow extra time in which to file a lawsuit on the grounds that since the patient (i.e., the child) is unable to think for himself, either in the sense of recognizing the injury or act of negligence or in deciding to seek compensation, some allowances should be made.

The variations in these specifications are even greater than those for adults, with some states holding to the same requirements as adults, while others vary widely from them. Table 2 lists the specifications for filing a malpractice suit when the injury has been suffered by a minor. Where a specification begins with "until," it should be read as "Statute of Limitations does not begin to run . . . until . . ."

TABLE 2. STATUTE OF LIMITATIONS FOR MINORS

Alabama	If under 4, until 8th birthday. Otherwise, adult law applies.
Alaska	2 years from discovery.
Arizona	If under 7, period begins at 7 or on death, whichever is first. Otherwise adult law applies.
California	Until 18 + 1 year.
Arkansas	3 years from occurrence or prior to 8th birthday, whichever is longer.
Colorado	If under 6, then two years after minor turns 6. Otherwise 2 years from discovery.
Connecticut	2 years from discovery.
Delaware	If under 6, then 3 years from occurrence or until he reaches age 6. Otherwise adult law applies.
Florida	2 years from discovery.
Georgia	Until 18 + 2 years.
Hawaii	Until 18 + 2 years.
Idaho	6 years from occurrence.
Illinois	Until 18 + 2 years.
Indiana	If under 6, until his 8th birthday. Otherwise adult law applies.
Iowa	Until 18 + 1 year.

Kansas	Until 18 + 1 year.
Kentucky	Until 18 + 1 year.
Louisiana	1 year from occurrence.
Maine	Until 18 + 2 years.
Maryland	Limitation period begins at 16.
Massachusetts	If under 6, until 9th birthday.
Michigan	Until 18 + 1 year.
Minnesota	Until 18 + 2 years.
Mississippi	Until 21 + 2 years.
Missouri	If under 10, until 12th birthday. Otherwise 2 years from occurrence.
Montana	Same as adult law.
Nebraska	2 years from occurrence.
Nevada	4 years from occurrence, but some exceptions.
New Hampshire	Until age 8 when 2-year limitation begins.
New Jersey	Until age 23.
New Mexico	Until 6 + 3 years. Otherwise adult law applies.
New York	10 years from discovery.
North Carolina	Until 18 + 1 year.
North Dakota	Until 18 + 1 year.
Ohio	If under 10, until 14th birthday. Otherwise adult law applies.
Oklahoma	Until 18 + 2 years.
Oregon	Until 18 + 1 year.
Pennsylvania	2 years from discovery.
Rhode Island	Until 16 + 1 year.
South Carolina	Until 18 + 1 year.
South Dakota	3 years from occurrence except: if child under 6, 2 years from 6th birthday.
Tennessee	Until 18 + 3 years.
Texas	If under 12, until 14th birthday. Otherwise, adult law applies.
Utah	2 years from discovery.
Vermont	Until 18 + 7 years.
Virginia	Until 18 + 2 years.
Washington	Until 18 + 3 years.
West Virginia	2 years from discovery.

Wisconsin	3 years from occurrence or until age 10, whichever is later.
Wyoming	Until 8th birthday or 2 years from occurrence, whichever is longer.
Dist. of Columbia	Until 18 + 3 years.

INDEX